Learning~Driven
SCHOOLS

A Practical Guide for Teachers and Principals

Barry Beers

Association for Supervision and Curriculum Development
Alexandria, Virginia USA

Association for Supervision and Curriculum Development
1703 N. Beauregard St. • Alexandria, VA 22311-1714 USA
Phone: 800-933-2723 or 703-578-9600 • Fax: 703-575-5400
Web site: www.ascd.org • E-mail: member@ascd.org
Author guidelines: www.ascd.org/write

Gene R. Carter, *Executive Director*; Nancy Modrak, *Director of Publishing*; Julie
Houtz, *Director of Book Editing & Production*; Ernesto Yermoli, *Project Manager*;
Georgia Park, *Senior Graphic Designer*; Keith Demmons, *Desktop Publishing
Specialist*; Dina Murray Seamon, *Production Specialist/Team Lead*

PAPERBACK ISBN-13: 978-1-4166-0346-7   ASCD product #106002   s6/06
PAPERBACK ISBN-10: 1-4166-0346-8

Also available as an e-book through ebrary, netLibrary, and many online book
sellers (see Books in Print for the ISBNs).

Quantity discounts for the paperback edition only: 10–49 copies, 10%; 50+ copies,
15%; for 1,000 or more copies, call 800-933-2723, ext. 5634, or 703-575-5634. For
desk copies: member@ascd.org.

Library of Congress Cataloging-in-Publication Data

Beers, Barry.
  Learning-driven schools : a practical guide for teachers and principals / Barry
Beers.
     p. cm.
  Includes bibliographical references and index.
  ISBN-13: 978-1-4166-0346-7 (pbk. : alk. paper)
  ISBN-10: 1-4166-0346-8 (pbk. : alk. paper) 1. Effective teaching. 2. Teachers—
In-service training. I. Title.

  LB1025.3.B44 2006
  371.1--dc22
                                        2006003537

15 14 13 12 11 10 09 08 07 06   1 2 3 4 5 6 7 8 9 10 11 12

To my wife, Shelley,
who has been my love and best friend
for over 38 years.
You continue to show me how
teaching is a calling, not just a job.
Living with an excellent
1st grade teacher causes me to never
lose sight of what is most important
in education—the love a teacher
has for her students.

To my three children,
Kelli, Lindsay, and Bryan. I love you
and am extremely proud of who you are
and what you have accomplished.
No parent could hope for
three more wonderful children.

And to my granddaughter, Jillian.
You bring a smile to my face every time
I think of you. I hope all of your teachers
are as caring and dedicated as those
I have had the pleasure of knowing.

Learning~Driven SCHOOLS

A Practical Guide for Teachers and Principals

Acknowledgments

During my career as an educator, I have taken many college courses, attended professional conferences, and read anything I could get my hands on that related to learning and teaching. I frequently talk to other principals to see what they are doing and thrive on new information that will help me do a better job. However, the main way I have learned about effective teaching is by watching effective teachers. Reading about instructional strategies is helpful, as is hearing presenters share their experiences, but nothing can compare with seeing good teaching in action.

It is because of this that I owe so much to the teachers at Tabb Middle School and York High School. Over the past 17 years, they have taught me about effective teaching. In this book, I have listed a few of the examples that I have witnessed. If a name is listed without a reference, it refers to a teacher whom I have observed. To list all of the teachers who have contributed to my learning would take much more space than this book will allow.

As a principal, I can only "experiment" with instructional strategies in a limited way. Practicing in faculty meetings, or presenting during professional development sessions, is certainly not the same as teaching a class of 30 teenagers (though there are many similarities). Therefore, I must rely on the expertise of teachers to frame my understanding of effective instruction as they transform theory into practice. The teachers in the two schools I mentioned have done a remarkable job and have been patient with some of my crazy ideas. In most cases, their reaction to my suggestions has been, "I am not too sure about that, but I will give it a try." Some of my suggestions have worked; some have not. In many situations, the teacher has "tweaked" the recommendation to make it more effective for her setting and teaching style. If I had teachers who were not willing to take risks and work toward continuous improvement, my own education would not have progressed. Therefore, I realize that any success I have as an educator is the result of the efforts of the many teachers who have "trained" me. I acknowledge them for that and appreciate all that they have done and continue to do.

I would also like to thank my superintendent, Dr. Steven Staples, for providing excellent leadership for my school division and me. His support and guidance have been extremely valuable as I have grown professionally over the years. Last, I would like to thank Ernesto Yermoli and Scott Willis of ASCD for providing direction and encouragement during the production of this book. They were able to challenge me to improve my product in a very positive and professional manner.

Introduction

For the past 20 years, I have observed more than a thousand classrooms. From these observations, I have reached some conclusions regarding the typical behaviors of teachers and administrators.

Teachers

Prior to instruction, teachers plan activities that they hope will engage their students and cover a certain amount of content, and then they list which local, state, or national curriculum standards will be covered. Some of the activities involve listening to teacher lectures, some are hands-on; sometimes students work alone, other times they work in pairs or in groups of three or four. Content usually is dictated by the textbook that the school district selected. Objectives typically describe what the students will do during a class period, not what knowledge and skills they will hopefully have by the end of the period.

During lecture, teachers periodically call on students who raise their hands, to ensure that students are paying attention and understand the material. Often, the students who answer the questions correctly knew the answers before class started. Questions posed to individual students during the class period are designed to validate that the teachers taught the material, not determine whether students learned it. During hands-on activities or group work, the teachers circulate around the room, answering individual questions and keeping the students on task. Homework is assigned to give students an opportunity to practice what they were expected to have learned at school.

After students are exposed to a week or two of input from a variety of sources, the teachers hold review sessions in which they prepare students for a quiz to be held the next day. This review often involves having students complete a worksheet that asks them to supply the information that will be covered by the quiz. Or, the teachers might call out questions directly related to the quiz. When students provide wrong answers, the teachers call on other students until one gives the correct response. They spend the same amount of time on questions that most students know as on questions that most don't. When the graded quizzes are returned, the teachers provide the correct answers to the questions, while students who missed the quiz sit in the hall.

This "teach and quiz" process is repeated one or more times until the unit or chapter is finished, after which the teachers spend another day of review in preparation for an upcoming test. The test review is similar to the quiz review, except that it covers more information. Tests, like quizzes, are based on what was taught. The test is graded and returned, and the teachers provide the correct answers to the questions. Students who did not perform well are encouraged to try harder next time or to start staying after school. They rarely do either.

And then it's on to the next unit or chapter.

The process of teaching typically occurs in isolation. Teachers rarely see one another inside the classroom, yet they all have opinions regarding who is a good teacher and who is not. Teachers of the same subject and grade often share materials but seldom discuss instructional strategies. Teachers of students in previous years don't share information with the students' current teachers, so the latter start the school year with no prior knowledge of their students' backgrounds. (The only exception is the occasional comment heard in the faculty lounge: "Boy, are you in for it next year.")

Administrators

The frequency and type of observations performed by administrators vary greatly. Some teachers report being observed once every three years, with a checklist placed in their mailboxes at the end of the year. Others say they are observed often and by a variety of people through announced and unannounced visits lasting from five minutes to the entire class period.

Observers typically look at teacher behaviors regarding instruction and at student behaviors regarding classroom management. Does the teacher use a variety of instructional techniques? Are the students on task? Is the objective of the class period's instruction written on the board? Does the teacher call on students randomly throughout the period? Is the information covered consistent with the local, state, and national curriculum standards?

Shortly after a formal observation, an administrator usually calls individual teachers to the office. To set the tone, the administrator offers the teacher a friendly greeting or perhaps an icebreaker and shares his thoughts regarding the effectiveness of the teacher's lesson. At the end of the conference, the administrator discusses with the teacher several areas of identified strengths, as well as areas in which improvement is needed. The administrator then gives the teacher a written evaluation. This evaluation might be in the form of a checklist that states whether certain conditions were evident, or it might be a rating based on a scale of specified criteria that labels the teacher as novice, intermediate, or advanced. Finally, the administrator might ask the teacher to share her thoughts about the lesson.

Often, both the teachers and the administrators are relieved when this process is over, because they have other things to do.

My goal in writing this book is to continue a conversation on a broader scale about a different process than the one I have described above. Outside the classroom, much discussion occurs regarding the importance of focusing on learning. Constructivism, differentiation, high-stakes assessments, backward design, teaching for understanding, assessment for learning, active learning, standards-based curriculum, authentic assessment—these are just some of the hot topics being discussed.

The problem, as I see it, is that many of these concepts are not making it into practice in the classroom. Teacher preparation programs focus on how to *teach*, not on how to help students *learn*. Teachers teach the way *they* were taught, but college professors are typically trained as researchers, not as teachers. Administrators observe processes, not products.

Good teachers handle their own problems, have few failures, and keep parents happy. This may have been acceptable in the past, but the current accountability movement has prompted the need for change. To graduate from high school, students must not merely pass tests based on the information a teacher deems to be important—they must demonstrate essential knowledge and skills. "Hobby teaching" (teachers choosing the curriculum based on their favorite topics) has succumbed to standardized testing. The "what" of teaching is no longer decided by individual teachers. It is only in the "how" that teachers can demonstrate their creativity and personal strategies.

All teachers should have daily objectives that are measurable and specific and lead to their accomplishing broad goals. Unit or guiding questions should lead to the discovery of answers to essential questions. No plan should have the same objective listed two days in a row in advance of the lesson. However, if mastery does not occur in the first lesson, the teacher may carry over the objective to the next day. Levels of understanding for *all* students should be checked prior to, during, and following instruction. Techniques to check group understanding should replace calling on the first students who raise their hands.

Teachers need a plan for students who "have it" before class starts. This plan should not consist of having them do work for another class or work more problems than the other students do.

Teachers also need a plan for those who don't "have it," one that applies both during and at the end of the class period. This plan should be more than, "Stay after class if you want additional help." In addition, teachers should plan prior to instruction how to assess students' progress based on the essential knowledge and skills identified by local, state, and national standards. Teacher collaboration should replace teacher isolation—teachers need to share their plans, materials, and best practices, and peer observation should be the norm.

To institutionalize these practices, administrators need to give teachers feedback based on their students' mastery of predetermined objectives. If students aren't learning, what difference does it make what strategies the teacher is using to teach? Administrators and other teacher trainers need to model effective instruction with an emphasis on learning. For example, principals who want to encourage their teachers to use active learning should engage teachers at the faculty meetings rather than lecture to them.

In the chapters that follow, I share some examples of how teachers can plan, teach, and assess for learning. I discuss how teachers and administrators can help turn "lecture halls" into "learning labs." I don't claim to have all the answers. In fact, I present my findings with the hope that others will comment and make suggestions about them that will increase my own understanding.

Years ago, as a novice administrator, I suggested some changes to a teacher. She informed me that she had been teaching for 30 years and didn't need my advice. My response was, "No, you have been teaching one year, 30 times." She had the skills to teach, but her technique had not changed as the students changed. The expression "If you always do what you have always done, you will always get what you have always gotten" is not true regarding learning and teaching. If we continue to use the same procedures year after year, we will get *less* than we have always gotten. To improve, we have to find a better way. We must change with the environment around us.

In this book, I begin with what is known about learning and let all discussion speak to that knowledge. In the first half, I discuss methods to plan, teach, and assess for learning. In the second half, I cover how administrators can create an emphasis on learning throughout the school. It also is important to note what this book is *not* about. My intent is not to provide a recipe that can be followed for perfect planning, instruction, and assessment. Having daily objectives does not mean emphasizing the memorization of basic facts to prepare for a test while ignoring a broader understanding of essential knowledge. Nor do I suggest that there is one best method for providing feedback to teachers. I do suggest, however, that there are certain guidelines that teachers and administrators can and should consider when making decisions about the learning process. The one factor that must drive all decisions is the student who sits in the third chair on the far right side of the class during second period, and the student in front of him, and so on. Both teachers and administrators need to be aware of how much each student is learning. That is what this book is about.

Although it might appear that I am overly critical of teachers and that I don't appreciate what they do, this is certainly not the case. I have been a teacher in one form or another all of my adult life. My wife and two daughters are teachers. I am amazed every day when I see the dedication and professionalism of the teachers around me. To so many of them, teaching is a calling, not just a job. What I *am* critical of is the *process* of teaching. I am critical of the current methods of teacher training and the process that administrators use to provide feedback to teachers. It's the traditional procedures we use that we need to examine, not the quality of the educators who use them. Our whole educational system has been designed to focus on *teaching*. It is now time to focus our efforts on *learning*.

The Study of Learning

1

Essential Question: What do we know about learning that can guide the way we educate our students?

To say "learning and teaching" is a bit awkward. "Teaching and learning" sounds better. This is because the focus in education traditionally has been on teaching first, then learning. If we could start over as educators with what we now know about learning, I doubt that our traditional strategies would dominate current practice. I have found that the biggest problem in changing instructional practice is that certain routines are too entrenched. We teach as we were taught. Even teachers new to the profession often rely on practices that hinder learning, not help it.

A consistent theme in this book is that we should focus on learning, not just on teaching. Therefore, we must look at the process of learning. How does it occur? What factors accelerate learning? What factors impede it? In this chapter, I first briefly investigate the history of the study of learning. Then I look at current theories regarding how learning occurs and at what I call "brain-based" theories of learning. I also explore various factors, such as motivation, stress, and feedback, that can affect learning.

A Brief History of Learning

"If learning is what we value," notes Jensen, "then we ought to value the process of learning as much as the result of learning" (1998, p. 16). A brief examination of the past sheds some light on why we should do this.

For much of human history, the process of learning was rather simple. People learned by finding someone who knew more than they did. They observed them and listened to them. Young boys watched their fathers hunt; young girls watched their mothers cook. Eventually, a guided apprenticeship model developed whereby children learned under the close supervision of an experienced craftsperson until they were ready to work on their own.

The Industrial Revolution changed this model. At that time, the "factory line" approach came to dominate theories about learning. The best way for learning to occur was via strict adherence to a prescribed process. Students were expected to follow certain rituals that had been proved effective. One reason for this practice was that education focused on reading, writing, and calculating at relatively low levels of application. However, those were the skills that were needed during that time.

Behaviorism

Behavior theorists focused on studying observable behaviors rather than studying mental activities. They suggested that the way to increase learning was through conditioning, which they classified as either *classic* or *operant*. An example of classic conditioning is Pavlov's famous experiment, in which dogs, having been conditioned to associate food with the ringing of a bell, would salivate upon simply hearing a bell ring. The idea is that certain stimuli will produce certain responses.

Operant conditioning involves providing a reward or punishment in response to a certain behavior. The probability of that behavior's reoccurring increases or decreases in the presence of reward or punishment. The prominent behaviorist B. F. Skinner (1953) demonstrated operant conditioning by training pigeons to perform certain tricks in response to the rewards they received. Teachers who use grades to stimulate students to perform well in their studies are employing behaviorist theory. A criticism of behaviorist theory is that it discounts the activities of the brain; that is, it does not explain how behavior changes and new learning occurs in the absence of rewards and punishments.

Social Cognition

Lev Vygotsky (1978) claimed that individual development depends primarily on the cultural environment that surrounds the learner; that is, it's a child's culture that dictates what and how that child learns. That culture includes the activities of parents, teachers, and siblings. Focusing on the child without understanding her culture provides only limited information to assist the child's intellectual growth. An example of this theory in action is the acquisition of language. Language is learned through interaction with others, and learning is advanced though the use of language.

A key part of Vygotsky's theory is his "Zone of Proximal Development." Here, he distinguishes between what students can do on their own versus what they can do with adult supervision or peer collaboration. Vygotsky claims that learning occurs in this zone. He suggests that decisions regarding curriculum, instruction, and assessment should consider the "actual" development of the child (what they can do on their own) and the "potential" development (what they can do with adult or peer assistance). In the social cognition model, it is the contribution of the adults and peers who determine the culture that causes changes within the zone of proximal development.

Developmental Stages and Cognitive Structures

Jean Piaget (1970), a contemporary of Vygotsky, offered the theory that children build cognitive structures, such as mind maps, depending on the stages of children's development. He described four cognitive structures, each corresponding to a particular age range of children:

- Sensorimotor (0 to 2 years of age).
- Preoperational (2 to 7 years of age).
- Concrete Operations (7 to 12 years of age).
- Formal Operations (12 to 15 years of age).

These cognitive structures change as children are exposed to their environments. Changes occur in relation to the previous situations that children experienced. Some experiences reinforce the cognitive structure of the child, and some change it. This constructivist view of learning was similar in nature for Vygotsky and Piaget.

Social Learning Theory

Albert Bandura is considered the leading proponent of this theory, which is a transition from behaviorist theory to cognitive structures theory. This theory, also called "observational learning theory," suggests that learning occurs through observing others in a social context, through the interaction of cognitive, behavioral, and environmental influences. Bandura concluded that reinforcement and punishment affect behavior but have only an indirect effect on learning (1977). For example, a student may observe cheating on a test by watching other students cheat. However, whether this observation affects that student's own behavior depends on how the student perceives the reward or punishment attached to the behavior.

The following four conditions must be present for social learning to occur:

- **Attention.** The learner must pay attention.
- **Retention.** The learner must remember what happened.

- **Motor reproduction.** The learner must be physically and intellectually capable of replicating the behavior.
- **Motivation.** The learner must want to replicate the behavior and believe that he is capable of doing so (Bandura, 1977).

Current Trends in Learning

Current trends in teaching focus more on how *much* students can learn than on how *best* they can learn. Learners process and perceive information in a variety of ways; the amount that they learn often depends on how the information is presented to them. Most learners can be classified in one of the following two main categories of learning styles:

- **Perceivers.** These learners are classified as either *concrete* or *abstract*. Concrete perceivers learn from direct experiences, such as from doing or acting. Abstract perceivers learn from indirect experiences, such as by observing and analyzing.
- **Processors.** These learners are classified as either *active* or *reflective*. Active processors use information as soon as they experience it. Reflective processors think about the information and use it accordingly.

In addition, we can examine learning styles by looking at the different approaches that students take to learning:

- **Visual learners.** These learners benefit when the teacher uses diagrams, charts, pictures, and videos. They often take detailed notes during the presentation of information.
- **Auditory learners.** These learners prefer discussions and lectures. They like text to be read aloud.
- **Tactile and kinesthetic learners.** These learners learn best by doing. They like to touch objects and move about in the classroom. They bore quickly during lectures.

Multiple Intelligences Theory

Howard Gardner (1983) describes eight ways that people understand the world around them and demonstrate their abilities intellectually. Each is a distinct "intelligence" that affects how we learn. He states that this list might not be exhaustive:

- **Verbal-Linguistic.** Involves the use of language.
- **Logical-Mathematical.** Involves the use of numbers and patterns, with reason and logic prevailing.
- **Visual-Spatial.** Involves the use of pictures and images to retain information.
- **Body-Kinesthetic.** Involves physical motion and interaction with space around the learner.
- **Musical-Rhythmic.** Involves sensitivity to tones and rhythm.
- **Interpersonal.** Involves the use of person-to-person relationships.
- **Intrapersonal.** Involves self-reflection and awareness.
- **Naturalistic.** Involves discrimination among living things.

For us to understand how people learn, Gardner suggests that we consider these eight intelligences. We must balance our curriculum to include, for example, the arts and movement intelligences, rather than addressing only verbal and mathematical intelligences. He suggests that we include activities such as cooperative learning, role playing, story telling, and musical performances as part of our daily instruction. Our assessments, too, should recognize the diversity of intelligences that exist.

Brain-Based Approaches to Learning

The amount of available information continues to increase rapidly and with it, the demand for critical thinking, problem solving, and reasoning. Today, merely memorizing and regurgitating acquired information is not enough. Educated people need to retrieve and process information and evaluate what information is valuable and what is not.

In the latter part of the 20th century, newly available technologies allowed researchers to study the brain and how learning occurs. Brain scanning techniques such as magnetic resonance imaging (MRI) and positron emission tomography (PET) gave us new ways to understand and see inside the brain. For the first time in history, we could analyze the brain while its owner was still alive. A new form of "inner science" developed (Bransford, Brown, & Cocking, 2000).

According to Bransford and colleagues, "Thirty years ago, educators paid little attention to the work of cognitive scientists, and researchers in the nascent field of cognitive science worked far removed from classrooms" (2000, p. 3). Now, cognitive and developmental psychologists are providing much data about teaching and learning based on extensive study inside and outside of the classroom. This information is divided into four categories, discussed in the sections that follow:

- Cognition
- Metacognition and feedback
- Motivation
- Individual and social factors

Cognition

Constructivism. Bransford and colleagues (2000) said that humans "come to formal education with a range of prior knowledge, skills, beliefs, and concepts that significantly influence what they notice about the environment and how they organize and interpret it. This, in turn, affects their abilities to remember, reason, solve problems, and acquire new knowledge. In the most general sense, the contemporary view of learning is that people construct new knowledge and understandings based on what they already know and believe" (p. 10). This means that people can build on pre-existing knowledge to facilitate the acquisition of new understandings. It also means that their prior knowledge might block the acquisition of new knowledge. For example, students who know that 8 is greater than 4 might have a hard time understanding that 1/4 is greater than 1/8. A student who has never been to the beach might have difficulty understanding an analogy in a story describing the pounding of the waves against the shore. A student who has never had pizza might have difficulty seeing pizza slices as metaphors for fractions.

According to Brooks and Brooks (1993), "We either interpret what we see to conform to our present set of rules for explaining and ordering our world, or we generate a new set of rules that better accounts for what we perceive to be occurring. Either way, our perceptions and rules are constantly engaged in a grand dance that shapes our understanding" (p. 4). This constructivist view suggests that learning is a search for meaning that is *contextual*. Learning is not isolated from the world around us; it *is* the world around us. All of the parts that we learn must be connected to the whole. Thus, learning should be personal and not merely the regurgitation of what someone else considers to be truth. Rather than retrieve an answer from memory, students must use their knowledge to synthesize the appropriate response. In other words, they must think!

Transfer of Learning. *Transfer* is the ability to extend what has been learned in one context to new contexts. All new learning involves transfer based on previous learning. Some kinds of learning experiences result in effective memory but poor transfer; others produce effective memory plus transfer. One factor that influences successful transfer is the degree of mastery of the original subject. Transfer also is affected by how much people learn, with understanding, rather than by their merely memorizing sets of facts or following fixed procedures. Learning disconnected pieces of information greatly reduces the possibility of transfer.

Transfer is further affected by the context of the original learning: People can learn in one context yet fail or be unable to transfer what was learned to other contexts. How tightly learning is tied to context depends on how the knowledge is acquired. More flexible transfer will occur if we highlight general principles that then can be applied to new situations. Students might have knowledge that is relevant to a learning situation, but that knowledge is not activated. They might misinterpret new information because of previous knowledge they use to construct new understandings. In addition, attempts to cover too much, too quickly, result in two situations that limit transfer: learning disconnected facts in the absence of relationships and learning relationships without specific knowledge of facts.

The ultimate goal of schooling is to help students transfer what they have learned in school to the everyday settings of home, community, and workplace. In John Dewey's vision, "School should be less about preparation for life and more like life itself" (Bransford et al., 2000, p. 77). However, this is not the case, as the following contrasts demonstrate. In schools,

- Much more emphasis is placed on individual work than in most other environments.
- The emphasis is on mental work, compared with everyday settings, in which there is a heavy reliance on the use of tools.
- Abstract reasoning is often emphasized, whereas in everyday settings contextualized reasoning is often stressed (Bransford et al., 2000; Resnick, 1987).

Memory. *Memory* is the result of the learning process that involves changes to our collection of knowledge and skills. Most memory is reconstructed and not merely a collection of archived data. It is categorized as *sensory*, *short-term*, or *long-term*. Sensory memory does not involve recognition and is stored automatically. For example, when we meet new people, we hear their names but we might not pay attention to them. This type of memory leaves our brains in a second or less. Thinking a bit about the name can put it in our short-term memory, which lasts less than a minute. We can remember the name for longer periods of time by saying it over and over, thereby placing it into long-term memory.

Long-term memory can be further divided into two categories: *explicit* and *implicit*. Explicit memory can have *semantic pathways* (for retrieval of facts, dates, textbook-type information) or *episodic pathways* (for memories based on a location or circumstance). Implicit memory can be *procedural* (motor or habit memory) or *reflexive* (automatic). Implicit memory implies that we know it; we just don't know we know it.

However, mere repetition does not keep information in our memory as long as adding meaning to it does. In this case, it becomes *associative*—that is, attached to something that is already embedded in our memories. We remember new information best when we can associate it. Associating a name with the person's occupation or age will cause the name to last longer in memory. The effectiveness of memory depends on such factors as attention, interest, emotion, and context.

Students today have learned more than they are able to demonstrate. The problem is often how we ask them to recall the information. Memories are either reconstructed as needed based on instructions that are in the brain, or brought to life based on signals that wake them up. Sometimes, the information students recall is "in the right church but the wrong pew," suggesting that a wrong mixture of information occurred. In other instances, the retrieval of information does not occur at the right time due to situational factors. For example, a student who fears failure will often focus on the result of not knowing, which interferes with his ability to retrieve the information that is needed to be successful. Or, the presence of distracters might limit the student's ability to focus. A girl who thinks she might be pregnant is likely to have difficulty focusing on her geometry test.

Metacognition and Feedback

Metacognition is the learner's ability to predict her performance on various tasks and to monitor her current level of mastery. Put simply, it involves "thinking about thinking." Successful learners are able to set goals, select appropriate strategies to meet those goals, and evaluate their progress along the way. If their progress is not what they would like it to be, they can adjust their strategies.

Having an understanding of how they learn helps students transfer effective practices from one situation to the next. "Transfer can be improved by helping students become more aware of themselves as learners who actively monitor their learning strategies and resources and assess their readiness for particular tests and performances" (Bransford et al., 2000, p. 67). For example, one student might learn best by skimming a chapter and then going back to pick up the details. Another student, thinking this a waste of time, might need to take copious notes during the first reading. In both cases, the students can only know what works best for them by reflecting on their learning process.

Reflection can arise from metacognition or can be guided by someone else, such as a teacher or a peer. Specific feedback reduces uncertainty, which reduces stress. Feedback that is specific, immediate, and includes nonverbals and choice is most effective. A smile is a nonverbal that is often remembered longer than verbal praise. Providing the student with various options regarding revisions gives the student ownership of the process and increases his acceptance of the feedback. Feedback from other students has positive effects because it provides variety and allows the students to interact socially. As Jensen notes, "When we feel valued and cared for, our brain releases the neurotransmitters of pleasure. This helps us enjoy our work more" (1998, p. 33). Sometimes, students who are confused by feedback from the teacher will completely understand when a peer makes similar comments.

Motivation

In the context of education, *motivation* refers to a student's desire or intent to learn. It can be subdivided into *intrinsic* and *extrinsic* forms. When students perform a task merely for its own sake, for the joy or feeling of accomplishment that results from its completion, or simply because it's the right thing to do, they are intrinsically motivated. Extrinsic motivation occurs because of an outside stimulus, such as the promise of a reward. Grades and stickers are examples of extrinsic motivators for students.

Jensen (1998) describes five key strategies to help students uncover their intrinsic motivation:

1. Elimination of threat
2. Goal-setting with some student choice on a daily basis
3. Positive reinforcement of students' beliefs about themselves and the learning, including affirmations, acknowledgment of success, and teamwork
4. Management of student emotions
5. Use of frequent feedback

Ideally, all students would be intrinsically motivated, but this is not the case. Sometimes, extrinsic forms of motivation must be used in order to build intrinsic motivation. Early attempts to motivate students involved extrinsic forms, a practice prompted by the work of behaviorists in the 1950s. However, although extrinsic rewards often work, they are most effective for menial tasks, not for assignments requiring higher levels of thinking. Most often, a combination of both intrinsic and extrinsic motivations is optimal.

The desire for learning is evident even in the absence of rewards. Novelty plays a key role in the motivation to learn. The mere pursuit of knowledge might be motivating by itself. Studies also show that sometimes students are capable of demonstrating higher levels of performance but are unmotivated to show it. Sometimes, a student's lack of motivation stems from the past (for example, a negative relationship with a previous teacher). The student who has always been unsuccessful in science is unlikely to walk into the chemistry lab on the first day of school ready to take on new challenges.

Sometimes, the lack of motivation stems from the present. Perhaps the student doesn't see the relevance of the course material to his everyday life. Or, maybe the teacher puts the student down in front of other students. Maybe the teacher's presentation style isn't conducive to the student's learning style.

The lack of motivation could also be related to the student's perception of the future. For example, a student who sees no connection between the curriculum and subsequent success in college or the workplace might not care about mastering the material.

Individual and Social Factors

Threats and Punishment. In attempting to control student behavior, teachers often use threats, such as of a loss of privileges, a time-out, detention, a lowered grade, a call to parents, or a trip to the principal's office. In many cases, these punishments do not change behavior. For example, sending a student from the room when he doesn't want to be there anyway could actually increase the frequency of the negative behavior. Lowering a struggling student's grade can take away any hope he may have of mastering the material.

Teachers often use threats and punishment against students they deem to be unmotivated. However, it's not that the students are unmotivated; it's just that they are motivated to do things other than what the teacher wants or expects. The skillful teacher motivates the students to increase their learning without threats or punishment.

On a biological level, threats increase stress, which can cause a loss of short-term memory. Chronic stress impairs the ability to prioritize events and can make students more prone to illness. "Students who have had early and constant childhood exposure to threat and high stress, particularly those who have come from families of violence, are often the ones for whom it is the most difficult to gain attention" (Jensen, 1998, p. 56). Students with high stress levels focus on survival. This limits their abilities to perform above the knowledge and comprehension levels expected for their grade. Whatever the reason, the skillful teacher must determine the conditions that must be addressed in order for students to succeed in the classroom.

A Challenging Environment. Learning is all about growing a better brain. Enrichment activities that cause this to happen are sometimes supplied for gifted learners but not for those perceived to be non-gifted. Research has shown, however, that many of these activities benefit all learners.

One key ingredient for enriching the brain is that the learning needs to be challenging. Novelty helps, but that alone is not enough if the experience is not challenging. "The single best way to grow a better brain is through challenging problem solving. This creates new dendritic connections that allow us to make even more connections" (Jensen, 1998, p. 35). Many capable students perform poorly because they are bored. Even when they see the relevance of gaining certain knowledge and skills, if the work is not challenging to them, they will often fail. Hunter (1982) suggests that tasks perceived to be too easy or too difficult do not motivate students. She notes that environments in which the level of concern (i.e., stress level) is either too high or too low will produce less than optimal results, so teachers should monitor these levels regularly.

Emotions. Neuroscientists have found that emotions play a large part in a student's ability and desire to learn. Previous thought was that emotions got in the way of learning. When students are asked why they failed a class, they rarely state that it was too hard. Rather, they state that they didn't like the teacher or the subject. As LeDoux says, "Emotions drive attention, create meaning, and have their own memory pathways" (Jensen, 1998, p. 72). Students can set personal goals, but how intensely they pursue those goals will depend on their emotions.

Biologists identify six emotions: joy (pleasure), fear, surprise, disgust, anger, and sadness. Early studies focused on pleasure and fear because those are the only emotions that we know how to measure (Jensen, 1998). As mentioned earlier in this chapter, emotions affect memory. Chemicals in the brain send a message when emotion confirms that the information being received is important; this process increases retention. Despite these findings, however, many traditional instructional practices ignore the role of emotions.

Meaning and Relevance. One way to reduce the stress of information overload is to add meaning to what is being learned. The type of meaning that is referred to is not a definition of terms but a relationship with the information. Relevance is not the same as meaning. For something to be meaningful there needs to be a connection to the everyday life of the individual. Learning how to change a tire on a car may be relevant for students with cars, but only meaningful when they have a flat tire. Many teachers assume that if something is relevant to the life of a student (the study of history, for example), it is also meaningful.

Meaning can also describe the level at which the information makes sense to the student. Graphic organizers such as mind maps, webs, outlines, and Venn diagrams can help students develop patterns for information that will help them understand the various relationships and develop meaning.

Attention Cycles. Getting and keeping the attention of their students is the main goal of many teachers. Recent research about the brain raises some questions about the effectiveness of some of the techniques we use to capture and hold students' attention. Getting the attention of students is often interpreted as getting the students to watch the teacher and not be distracted by other stimuli. Some teachers feel that if students listen to them enough, and do so attentively, they will learn.

Blood flow to the human brain constantly changes, affecting students' attention and ability to learn. This change in the flow of blood causes high- and low-attention cycles that occur approximately 16 times in a 24-hour period. At night, this is referred to as light sleep or deep sleep. During the day, our brains are either aroused or resting, or somewhere in between these two conditions. If students are drowsy, they might be at the bottom (resting stage) of their attention cycles. Movement is a good remedy for this situation. Research has shown that lower test scores result at certain times in the students' attention cycles (Jensen, 1998). This is why "one-shot" tests are not as effective as portfolios, which look at achievement in a variety of ways over a period of time.

However, paying constant attention in class can also inhibit learning. This is because students cannot make meaning of the information while it is being presented. As Jensen (1998) notes, "First, much of what we learn cannot be processed consciously; it happens too fast. We need time to process it. Second, in order to create new meaning, we need internal time. Meaning is always generated from within, not externally. Third, after each new learning experience, we need time for the learning to 'imprint'" (p. 46). Simply put, the presentation of new material is external, and making meaning of it is internal.

Teachers sometimes complain that some of their students are inattentive. This is not an accurate description. All students are paying attention to something; the object of their attention simply might not be what the teacher desires. The successful teacher monitors students' attention and develops strategies to guide that attention in the appropriate direction.

With all that we know about how students learn, why do we allow traditional practices such as lecturing and note copying to dominate our classrooms? Why do we continue to focus on activities, rather than on student mastery of learning objectives? Why do we emphasize coverage of content while ignoring the characteristics of students? In the chapters to follow, I discuss some alternatives to these practices.

What's the Point?

- Early studies about learning focused on how various external stimuli affected people's behaviors.
- Because of improvements in technology, learning is now studied in relation to changes in the brain, thereby advancing the findings from speculation to science.
- How well we learn depends on what we already know and how we feel during the time of learning.
- Learners demonstrate intelligence in a variety of ways.

2

Planning for Learning

Essential Question: How can teachers plan for learning so that each student reaches his maximum potential?

What gets planned, gets done. One reason teaching hasn't changed much during the last century is because planning hasn't changed. Many teachers pull out the same plans and transparencies year after year. In fact, some teachers purposely don't list dates for their plans because doing that would require alterations in the future. The only change from the past is that rather than fill up the squares in a green planning book, some teachers now use binders containing plans that are prepared in word processing programs. Unfortunately, the only time plans change is when a new textbook is adopted. I overheard one teacher share that she had been teaching so long, she didn't need to plan. I wonder: Would we hire a contractor to build our house who said he didn't bother with blueprints because he had it all in his head and planned to build the house the same way he built houses 20 years ago?

Teacher preparation programs typically provide training in the practice of writing lesson plans. Prospective teachers are told that objectives must be specific and measurable and include a variety of activities that will keep the students engaged. Assessment should be related to accomplishing the objective. During the initial phase of their training and practicum, student teachers typically spend long hours completing very detailed plans, which the supervising teacher periodically reviews. Some time between the initial training experience and the first year of teaching, the emphasis on planning changes.

Teachers new to a building quickly sense their surroundings and make decisions based on their findings. If no one around them finds it necessary to plan, new teachers find other ways to use their time, which is extremely limited in the first year of teaching. Planning time becomes copying time, or grading time, or miscellaneous paperwork time. Teachers learn to survive, and planning gets put on the back burner.

Because time is so limited, both new and veteran teachers are using the Internet to find lesson plans that other teachers have found effective. Many sites provide detailed lesson plans for a variety of subjects and grade levels. In order to gain an awareness of what these sites offer, I visited the top 10 that resulted from a search for the phrase "lesson plans." According to one site, "Many lesson plans don't necessarily need an assessment." (Good plans do.) Another said, "Just before moving on to the assessment phase, you should have some sort of closure for the lesson plan." (This person obviously hadn't heard of assessment for learning.) Among the objectives listed on the sites were the following:

- "Students will learn about the geography of the Midwest." (A little broad, don't you think?)
- "Participate in a debate about the pros and cons of nationalism." (This is an activity, not an objective.)
- "Incorporate map reading, math, library research skills, and writing." (To do what?)
- "Demonstrate that students value their peers' contributions by quietly listening while their peers are speaking." (Does this mean that as long as they are quiet, they have mastered the objective?)

- "Understand the three main kinds of rocks: sedimentary, metamorphic, and igneous." (How do you understand a rock?)

Many of the lesson plans didn't even list any objectives. Some plans started with "concepts taught." Quite often, the assessment listed didn't measure the objective. In one example, the objective was that the students demonstrate the correct way to shoot a basketball, and the assessment was based on how many baskets they made during a game. A proper assessment would assess much more than shooting technique (in any case, students can make baskets by using very poor technique).

The one part of the plan that was consistent in all examples was the description of very detailed activities. The examples I found on the Internet are typical of most plans: They are filled with activities that identify what the students will *do*, not what and how they will *learn*. Later in this chapter, I discuss "learner plans" that focus on what the students will be able to do, how they will be engaged in learning, and how they will demonstrate their mastery of the objectives.

Teachers and administrators who want to focus on learning, not just teaching, should start with planning. Teachers have to plan for learning, not for teaching. As Harry and Rosemary Wong (1998) suggest, "Stop asking, 'What am I going to cover tomorrow?' 'What video am I going to show?' 'What worksheet am I going to give out?' 'What activity am I going to do?' Danger lurks in the word *I*. Start asking, 'What are my students to learn, achieve, and accomplish tomorrow?'" (p. 209).

No longer do teachers have complete freedom to choose which topics they will teach in their courses. Today, the curriculum (that is, the path to run) is decided by national, state, and district standards. I have explained to my faculty that the "what" isn't up to them; it's the "how" that teachers control, taking into consideration the unique characteristics of the students they have in their classes. The creativity and personal strengths of the teacher can be demonstrated in the "how." No longer can textbooks dictate planning. A red flag should go up if a teacher says, "Today we are covering Chapter 6."

Backward Design

Wiggins and McTighe (1998) suggest a "backward design" for planning. They suggest starting with the end—that is, the accomplishment of identified goals and objectives—in mind. The curriculum becomes "the evidence of learning" (p. 8) that is called for by the standard. Another component of backward design is that assessments are planned at the beginning of the unit. The teacher, not the textbook publisher, develops the assessments. The assessments should reflect the essential knowledge and skills that relate to the identified standard. The teacher must determine what would be considered acceptable evidence that the standard has been met.

The accountability movement has received much criticism from some educators and members of the general public. Some feel that high-stakes testing has caused teachers to "teach to the test." In doing so, they cause their students to memorize disconnected trivia rather than gain an understanding of larger concepts. The critics say that our curricula are a mile wide and an inch deep. Some state that life isn't a multiple-choice test. While this may be the case in some classrooms, knowing facts and having deep understandings can be accomplished together if the teacher keeps the big picture in mind. Deep understanding can't occur without specific facts, and knowing specific facts isn't useful in the absence of a greater understanding that ties those facts together to add meaning for the learner.

Wiggins and McTighe (1998) distinguish between two types of curriculum-framing questions: unit questions and essential questions. They describe unit questions as being "more subject- and topic-specific, and therefore better suited for framing particular content and inquiry" (p. 44). Unit questions lead to more subtle essential questions. For planning purposes, I think of these types of questions as *objectives* (unit questions) and *goals* (essential questions): A goal should state that students are able to answer essential questions, and an objective should state that students can answer unit questions. Goals relate to the general understanding of concepts. They can't be accomplished in specific lessons; rather, they should identify essential understandings to be accomplished over time. Objectives are more specific, identifying what should happen on a daily basis.

Prior to developing a plan, teachers need to identify what understanding looks like. Wiggins and McTighe (1998) list six facets of understanding. According to them, when we truly understand, we can do the following:

- **Explain:** Provide thorough, supported, and justifiable accounts of phenomena, facts, and data.
- **Interpret:** Tell meaningful stories; offer apt translations; provide a revealing historical or personal dimension to ideas and events; make ideas personal or accessible through images, anecdotes, analogies, and models.
- **Apply:** Effectively use and adapt what we know in diverse contexts.
- **Have perspective:** See and hear points of view through critical eyes and ears; see the big picture.
- **Empathize:** Find value in what others might find odd, alien, or implausible; perceive sensitively on the basis of prior direct experience.
- **Have self-knowledge:** Perceive the personal style, prejudices, projections, and habits of mind that both shape and impede our own understanding; be aware of what we don't understand and why understanding is so hard.

To thoroughly understand, a student needs to go beyond repeating facts that the textbook provides. He needs to be able to justify his position based on a collection of data and the application of concepts and principles. He needs to be able to explain how and why.

An example of the connection between goals and objectives can be demonstrated by standard CE.2a of the 2001 Virginia

Standards of Learning for Civics and Economics (Commonwealth of Virginia Board of Education, 2001, p. 2), which lists the following goals and objectives:

Essential Understanding: Fundamental political principles define and shape American constitutional government.

Essential Question: What are the fundamental political principles that have shaped government in the United States?

Essential Knowledge: Fundamental political principles:

- *Consent of the governed.* People are the source of any and all governmental power.
- *Limited government.* Government is not all-powerful and may do only those things people have given it the power to do.
- *Rule of law.* The government and those who govern are bound by the law.
- *Democracy.* In a democratic system of government the people rule.
- *Representative government.* In a representative system of government people elect public officeholders to make laws and conduct government on their behalf.

Essential Skills:

- Examine and interpret primary and secondary source documents (CE.1a)
- Distinguish between relevant and irrelevant information (CE.1d)

The *goal* for the unit would be the Essential Understanding. The *daily objectives* would be the attainment of the Essential Knowledge and Essential Skills listed.

Wiggins and McTighe (2004) suggest teachers ask WHERETO when they are planning their lessons:

- The "W" asks the teacher to decide how she will help the students know *where* they are headed and *why*.
- The "H" suggests that the teacher ask herself how she will *hook* the students to get and keep their attention.
- The first "E" asks the teacher to determine how she will *engage* her students in answering the big questions.
- The "R" asks the teacher to decide how she will provide time for students to *reflect* and allow them opportunities to *revise* and *refine* their work.
- The second "E" asks how the students will *exhibit* their understanding and how they will receive feedback through self, peer, or teacher evaluation.
- The "T" asks how the teacher will *tailor* the instruction to meet her students' various needs.
- And finally, the "O" asks how students can *organize* their learning experiences so that understanding is reached.

Teachers who answer the WHERETO questions while planning will be well on their way to having their students demonstrate mastery of important knowledge and skills.

To have teachers help each other with planning, I launched three experiments by asking certain groups of teachers to plan together for the common courses they taught. The first time I asked teachers to plan a unit together, the results were eye-opening. I discovered that it was difficult for them because they all had their own favorite activities that they didn't want to give up. They couldn't agree on the assessment because their activities were so varied.

I asked another group to develop a unit test by starting with the essential knowledge that was identified in the curriculum guide. This took a great deal of time because they weren't able to use many of their old test questions. What they found was that many of the old test items didn't match the essential knowledge that was required. After they developed the test, they planned the activities. The result of developing this new unit test was that some activities were short-ened or thrown out and new activities were added.

I had a third group identify the test question(s) that related to each daily objective. My purpose in doing this was to have the teach-ers match what they needed to assess with their daily objectives for student learning. After students took the test, I asked the teachers to identify areas in which students did poorly and then to go back to the activities of the days in which those areas were covered to see why this occurred.

The result of these three experiments was that many teachers saw that in many cases, there was no clear connection between what students needed to be able to do, the activities they were engaged in, and how they were assessed.

Objectives

From the three experiments discussed above, I also discovered that some teachers either didn't attempt to write or didn't know how to write specific, behavioral objectives. In post-observation conversa-tions, the teacher and I discuss the objective of the lesson more than any other part. Identifying exactly what it is that the teacher wants the students to be able to learn is hard work. It's also the most important part of planning. Assigning activities that don't guide the students toward the accomplishment of the objective doesn't make good use of the scarce time that's available. Often, the teacher and I spend a long time trying to identify what the students truly need to be able to do. We then analyze the activities that occurred. I might ask, "If that was your true objective, would you have your students spend-ing 20 minutes doing this?" And the teacher might respond, "No, I would have them spend only 5 minutes with that and would use the other 15 minutes having them do this."

Teachers often say that there isn't enough time to teach every-thing. I agree. However, I have found that there is time to have stu-dents master very specific objectives when all activities are designed with this in mind. Much time is wasted every day with "nice" activities that students enjoy and that keep them busy.

Research has shown that "the effective classroom appears to be the one in which the students are kept aware of instructional objectives and receive feedback on their progress toward those objectives" (Wise and Okey in Wong & Wong, 1998, p. 211). New teachers often ask me if I want to see the objective written on the board. I tell them that this is a good practice but helpful only if the objective is shared with the students. To have it copied on a board in the back of the classroom that no one ever sees is a waste of time. Teachers should inform students of what they will learn each day and why the learning is important. They should refer to the objective before, during, and at the conclusion of the class period. For the objective to lead to student learning, certain criteria must be evident.

Objectives should state what "the students will be able to" (TSWBAT) do by the end of the class period. Some teachers say that certain objectives take multiple days to accomplish. This is especially common in elective courses. Does this mean that the students don't have to learn anything the first two days of a three-day objective? I have never seen a good objective that couldn't be broken down into daily segments. Forcing teachers to develop daily objectives that don't repeat causes them to break down learning into chunks—and combining learning chunks with time to reflect increases attention and memory, as discussed in Chapter 1.

Art teacher Karen Woodward initially had four- to five-day objectives because it took that long for students to finish their projects and she allowed them to work at their own pace. She also had students who got behind. Some of these stayed after school to complete their work; others took lowered grades or zeros. When she developed daily objectives that were shared with her students (for example, "Today you need to complete the rough draft of the drawing in pencil so that you can add color tomorrow"), they were better able to keep up and meet more deadlines.

Math teacher Stephanie Singletary had previously listed "calculate the area of irregular figures using rectangles and triangles" as a three-day objective. When challenged to break it down, she was able to identify the necessary skills that students needed each day to accomplish the task. The acquisition of these skills became the daily objective. Without daily objectives, teachers often postpone assessments until the end of the unit. What happens on day four when the teacher realizes that students haven't mastered the objective? There's not enough time to go back, so the teacher moves on to the next set of objectives.

Objectives should state the expected learning, not the activities that will occur. "The students will read about Abraham Lincoln" is not a learning objective unless the students will be learning how to read. "The students will watch a movie about the Civil War" is a learning objective only if the teacher is going to show the students how to watch a movie.

A key part of the objective is the verb that is used to word it. Providing lists of verbs (see Figure 2.1) that identify various levels of learning can greatly help teachers write good objectives. Objectives should list the behavior that demonstrates the learning that is to occur. "Understand" and "appreciate" apply to goals, not to objectives. "Learn," "know," and "review" are other words that shouldn't be used in phrasing objectives.

In most cases, adding the *conditions* and *criteria* for the objective makes it more meaningful. For example, rather than "TSWBAT read a map," the objective could be worded, "Given a Virginia map (condition), TSWBAT list the best directions for driving from Roanoke to Williamsburg that require no travel on interstate roads (criterion)." Teachers should take care not to add too much to the objective, as this might make it difficult to understand.

All plans should list the national, state, or district standards that relate to the objective of the day. With some standards, it's possible to be very specific; for example, a Virginia mathematics standard

FIGURE 2.1
Verbs to Use When Phrasing Objectives

Level of Learning	Verbs That Relate to the Level
Evaluation	appraise, assess, choose, compare, conclude, decide, defend, discriminate, explain, evaluate, give your opinion, judge, justify, measure, prioritize, rank, rate, select, test
Synthesis	change, combine, compose, construct, create, design, formulate, generate, integrate, invent, plan, prepare, predict, pretend, produce, rearrange, reconstruct, reorganize, revise, substitute, visualize, write
Analysis	analyze, categorize, classify, compare, contrast, debate, deduct, diagnose, diagram, differentiate, distinguish, examine, explain, infer, order, separate, specify
Application	apply, calculate, compute, conclude, construct, demonstrate, determine, discover, draw, examine, illustrate, make, operate, show, solve, use
Comprehension	contrast, convert, describe, discuss, estimate, explain, interpret, paraphrase, put in order, restate, rewrite, summarize, trace, translate
Knowledge	define, identify, label, list, locate, match, memorize, name, quote, recall, spell, state, tabulate

states, "Write deductive arguments as well as coordinate and algebraic demonstrations that triangles are congruent." Other standards, which are more general in nature, cover many objectives, such as a Virginia English standard that states, "Give short presentations based on literature, personal topics, and research." It's not necessary to list every standard that has anything to do with the objective of the day. To list 8.2, 8.4, 8.7, and 9.3 as the standards for one class period's objective is a waste of time. Other examples of what I consider to be acceptable objectives include the following:

- Use properties, postulates, and theorems to determine whether two lines are parallel.
- Write numerals, using a base-10 model or picture.
- Identify and differentiate the six types of simple machines.
- Draw a straight line through a set of experimental data points, and determine the slope.

- Use clues in a paragraph to predict what might happen in the remainder of the chapter.
- Critique the presentation of a speaker by analyzing his content, voice, and body language.
- Locate and describe the geographical regions of North America.
- Analyze a political cartoon, and discuss how the intended audience would react to it.
- Execute simple commands given in Spanish.

Assessment

Once the teacher has determined the goals and objectives that students need to accomplish, her next step should be to identify the assessments that will validate the accomplishment of the intended outcomes. This is not how teachers typically operate. Often, the assessment is determined *after* activities are planned and in many cases near the completion of the unit. When textbooks and favorite activities dictate planning, assessments follow in line. Standards are considered only as they relate to what has already been planned.

Planning also should include the assessment *of* learning (formal unit quizzes and tests at the end of instruction) and assessment *for* learning (informal checking during instruction). Typically, assessment for learning isn't planned. I discuss this method of assessment in detail in Chapter 4.

Further, planning should include how differentiated instruction will occur. Checking for prior knowledge may indicate that some students have all the knowledge and skills they need to complete a task, whereas others may be severely lacking. In addition to their readiness levels, students differ in their interests and how they learn most effectively. The teacher must provide different paths for students in order for them to all have an equal opportunity to master the objective. Much information is available to teachers regarding methods for differentiating instruction. A good place to start is Carol

Ann Tomlinson's 1999 book, *The Differentiated Classroom: Responding to the Needs of All Learners.*

Teachers should be given templates that include the key ingredients for plans but allow them the flexibility to alter the format according to their individual preferences. Figure 2.2 shows an example of a template developed by Terry Payne that is different from most traditional plans. It's a *learner* plan because it emphasizes what the learner will do, not what the teacher will do. (Additional learner plans are in Appendixes A and B.)

Unit Plans

Unit plans should guide the development of daily lesson plans. In the example in Figure 2.3, the daily objectives are listed along with the specific test questions that assess each objective. This unit plan was developed by English teachers Amy Mule', Erin McGrann, and Lynda Fairman prior to developing daily lesson plans that identified the activities for each day. (Additional unit plans are in Appendixes C, D, and E.)

Some teachers may balk at the need to write plans with specific objectives. However, my experience tells me that, for most teachers, this is one of the areas needing greatest improvement. As I mentioned earlier in this chapter, when new teachers see that veteran teachers don't do extensive planning, they soon abandon what they did as student teachers. The expectation of the administration has a great impact on planning. In many schools, plans are never shared with anyone. However, in schools that have an emphasis on learning, plans are checked regularly as part of the observation process, or periodically throughout the year. By collecting all plans one day in the fall and one day in the spring, my assistant principals and I are able to get a clear picture of how teachers plan for learning to occur in their classrooms. It takes a full day for each of us, but the time is well spent in my opinion. We also check the plans during all classroom observations.

FIGURE 2.2

Sample Learner Plan for Life Sciences

Title: Introduction to Scientific Method		**Content Area:** Life Science
Grade Level: 7	**Date:** April 10, 2005	**SOL:** LS 1

Lesson Objectives: The student will be able to (TSWBAT) • Explain the importance of asking questions in life science. • Identify the steps of the scientific method. • Relate the steps of the scientific method to real life.	**Daily Challenge:** What piece of equipment is used for measuring volume and liquids? *(graduated cylinder)*

Check for Prior Knowledge: How many of you can describe the scientific method?

Student Engagement:

 Bell Ringer: Students will write three questions about the natural world. Think/pair/share.

1. Students close their eyes and imagine a life scientist. "What do you see?" Look at page 7 in the book. Discuss the people at the top of the page. "Who can become a scientist?" "Why ask questions?"
2. Imagine that your class is on a field trip to a wildlife refuge. On the trip, you discover several deformed frogs. The deformities include extra limbs, malformed or missing limbs, and facial malformations. What could have caused the deformities? Working with your partner, discuss what could have caused the deformities. (2 minutes)
3. Discuss possible answers with the teacher.
4. Watch PP on scientific method and write steps.
5. Discuss how the scientific method could be used to find out why the frogs are deformed. (Refer to page 15.)
6. Students check with their partners to make sure they have written the steps of the scientific method. SWD will receive back-up notes as needed.
7. Put the steps of the scientific method in order using strips.

Homework: Define vocabulary words in notebook: life science, scientific method, hypothesis, controlled experiment, variable, data

(Figure continued on next page)

Developing good plans takes time. The small amount of time that teachers are given is often taken up with phone calls, parent conferences, copying, grading, and everything else except planning. I suggest to all teachers that they put their daily and long-range plans

FIGURE 2.2 *(cont.)*
Sample Learner Plan for Life Sciences

Assessment of Learning (Formal)		Assessment for Learning (Informal)		Resources		Differentiation
Check and correct homework	x	Observation	x	Science text		Cooperative learning
Student drill	x	Walk around		Microscope		Varied grouping
Quiz		Signaling		Computers		Adjustment for readiness
Test		Choral response		Flex camera		Choice provided
Presentation		Class work	x	Overhead		Movement
Project	x	Oral questioning		Manipulative	x	Manipulatives
Written report		Discussion		TV/VCR		Contract
Other:		Whiteboards		PowerPoint		Peer editing
		Flash cards		Lab equipment		Stations
		Other (interactive notes):		Other:	x	Think/pair/share
						Other:

Power Strategies				Recommendations/ Observations for Future Use
Setting objectives and providing feedback	x	Note taking and summarizing		
Questions, cues, and advance organizers		Reinforcing effort and providing recognition		
Identifying similarities and differences	x	Generating and testing hypotheses	x	
Cooperative learning		Homework and practice		
Nonlinguistic representations				

Source: Terry Payne.

in a Word document that can be tweaked from year to year rather than reinvented. I would rather have them spend the time evaluating the plan than writing it down. This also takes time. However, if the teacher is able to get, say, 20 plans recorded digitally the first year and then 30 more the next, before long all of her plans for the entire year will be recorded. Having teachers plan together (as discussed in Chapter 8) greatly facilitates this process.

FIGURE 2.3
Sample Unit Plan for English

SOL	Test Question Number	TSWBAT
7.3a M (4/19)	1-10	Identify a variety of propaganda techniques.
7.3a T (4/20)	31-40	• Analyze a variety of media, print and nonprint, for types of propaganda. • Identify effective word choice from the different types of media that persuade the audience.
7.3b W (4/21)	11-20	Distinguish between fact and opinion in spoken and written communication.
7.3c 7.4c 7.6d, e Th (4/22)	21-30	• Define *connotation, denotation,* and *viewpoint.* • Determine if wording in sentences and in various media examples is connotative or denotative. • Generate original examples of connotative word meanings.
7.3c 7.4c 7.6e F (4/23)	21-30	• Explore the emotional and experiential content of word connotation and viewpoint. • Contrast the denotative meaning of a word with its various connotative meanings. • Explore how connotation and viewpoint are used in media and persuasion to evoke powerful associations in readers and listeners.

Source: Amy Mule', Erin McGrann, and Lynda Fairman.

We have also found success asking "computer moms" to help with this process. Many parents are willing to volunteer but don't want to embarrass their children by being visible at school. At the beginning of the year, parents (usually moms) volunteer to help by creating word processing documents at home. When a teacher wants her plans put into a Word document, I send copies home with the child of the volunteer. After entering the plans, the parent e-mails the document back to me to share with the teacher.

I have never seen an effective lesson that wasn't well planned in advance. Planning for activities is easy; planning for learning is not. However, once a teacher gets in the habit of starting with an appropriate objective and determining assessments prior to identifying activities, planning for learning gets easier.

Although planning for learning is essential, it's merely what's recorded on paper. The next chapter deals with what's most important—teaching for learning.

What's the Point?

- Attention to planning is strong during teacher preparation but often declines after that.
- Typical lesson plans identify what the teacher will do and are dictated by former practice or the sequence of material in the textbook.
- Learner plans should identify what students will learn, how they will learn, and how the teacher will determine what they learned.
- Teaching will not change until planning does.

Teaching for Learning

3

Essential Question: What teaching strategies make the best use of what we know about how people learn?

Chapter 1 discussed research regarding how people learn. This research came from cognitive and developmental psychologists and the emerging field of neuroscience. There's no shortage of information regarding this topic; the problem is that much of what we do in schools ignores this research. Brooks and Brooks (1993) list five conditions that exist in many classrooms today that are impediments to learning:

- The U.S. classroom is dominated by teacher talk.
- Most teachers rely heavily on textbooks.
- Students are encouraged to work in isolation on tasks that require low-level skills, rather than higher-order reasoning.
- Student thinking is devalued in most classrooms. Teachers seek to enable students to know the "right" answer.
- Schooling is premised on the notion that there exists a fixed world that the learner must come to know.

Constructivism

The solution, according to Brooks and Brooks and many others, is that teachers need to become constructivists; that is, "in the classroom, they must provide a learning environment where students search for meaning, appreciate uncertainty, and inquire responsibly" (1993, p. v).

There are five overarching principles of constructivist pedagogy:

- Posing problems of emerging relevance to learners
- Structuring learning around "big ideas" or primary concepts
- Seeking and valuing students' points of view
- Adapting curriculum to address students' suppositions
- Assessing student learning in the context of teaching (Brooks & Brooks, 1993)

The constructivist point of view suggests that we construct our own understanding of the world in which we live. Sometimes, what we see makes sense to us based on our previous understandings; at other times, it's not consistent with what we understand, so we either alter it to fit our set of rules or change our set of rules to acknowledge this new information. Learning is not discovering more, but rather interpreting through a different scheme or structure (Brooks & Brooks, 1993). The goal for students is not to repeat what the teacher or textbook has provided but to internalize the information that's around them so that they can generate their own meaning.

Piaget was one of the best-known advocates for constructivism. He described scientific thought as a dynamic process of continual construction and reorganization. However, his findings were not readily accepted by educators. In contrast, the work of behaviorists such as Skinner (1953) and Thorndike and Stein (1937) described human behavior as a stimulus-response relationship. The suggestions that follow in this chapter are consistent with a constructivist point of view.

Checking for Prior Knowledge

In traditional teaching, it's not necessary to check for prior knowledge. If the objective is to teach Chapter 5 or to teach the causes of the Civil War, it's not important what knowledge the students have upon entering the classroom. At the end of the class period, the teacher can proudly say, "I taught it." The assumption is that the student is an empty vessel that the teacher will fill. However, if the objective is to have students learn, checking for prior knowledge is essential. Learner-centered environments pay close attention to the knowledge, skills, attitudes, and beliefs that learners bring to the educational setting. As stated in Chapter 1, the knowledge that students bring to the learning environment may help or hinder the acquisition of new knowledge or the performance of a new skill.

One teacher asked, "What if I check to see how well the students can master the objective at the beginning of class and find out that some can already do it?" This teacher is ready to discuss differentiated instruction. Unfortunately, many students sit through classes bored because they have already mastered the skill that's being taught. The traditional solution for many gifted students is to give them more to do, rather than challenge them to explore other perspectives or take on more complex tasks.

The method used to check for prior knowledge can be very simple and should take no more than five minutes. Students may write their responses, but the teacher should use techniques that allow her to quickly assess the group without getting caught in a blizzard of collecting and grading papers. Some examples:

- "Write down everything you know about communism."
- "Look at the chart on the board comparing and contrasting various religions according to five criteria. How many of you can fill in five of the squares? Ten? All fifteen?"

- "Think about the debate last night for a few minutes, and then share your thoughts with your neighbor. Be prepared to tell us who your neighbor thought won the debate and why."

This think-pair-share technique is an excellent way to check for prior knowledge in a nonthreatening manner.

Checking for prior knowledge not only gives the teacher valuable information regarding the knowledge and skills students bring to the class; it also prepares the students for the lesson to follow. Differentiated instruction responds to the readiness and interests of the students. How can the teacher make informed decisions about learning and teaching without this information?

Metacognition

Metacognition is often referred to as *active learning*. Using metacognition, the student learns to take control of his own learning. He sets goals and monitors his progress along the way. Much attention is given to the process that he uses to gain new knowledge and skills. Assessing for prior knowledge is a form of metacognition; students should receive feedback about their current status in regard to future learning goals. Teachers who encourage metacognition often use peer editing and reciprocal teaching. Initially, the teacher will structure the activities and monitor the feedback, but eventually the students should take more control of the process. Students achieve more when they reflect upon their work and the work of others.

Teachers should pose questions to students such as, "How did you reach that conclusion?" "Which advance organizer works best for you?" "What emotions caused you to react to the story the way you did?" Assessment for learning (which I discuss in Chapter 4) involves both the student and the teacher in knowing where the student is at that moment, how she got there, and what she needs to do to move forward successfully.

Predicting is also a form of metacognition—the student decides what information she has and how she can use it to develop a hypothesis. Teachers should encourage their students to predict by asking questions: "What do you think will happen next in the story and why?" "If I mix these two substances together, what do you think will happen?" The key to making this work is to allow students to analyze their predictions at the end of the event. Whether they were correct or mistaken is not as important as the process they used to make the predictions and the reflection that follows.

Transfer

One of the best ways to promote transfer of knowledge to other subjects and to the real world is to present information in multiple contexts: "You have learned how to find the area of a rectangle. How would you decide how much paint is needed to cover the back wall of this classroom?" "How would you decide how much wrapping paper is needed to cover this box?" Another way is to allow students to use "tools of the trade": "This plum bob is what a carpenter uses to align a board properly. What other uses of this device can you think of?" "A doctor uses a stethoscope like this one to listen to the heart. How do you think it works?"

In order for students to learn to transfer, information should be presented in small chunks followed by some activity that allows the students to internalize it. The processes of acquiring new information and internalizing that information can't occur at the same time, so practice sessions should follow short periods of input. Students must receive frequent feedback so that misconceptions don't block future learning. Many teachers who try to rush through the content to get it covered find that they must reteach it the next day because the students didn't get it the first time. In some cases, they get negative results when they give the test a few days later; by then it's too late to go back, so they move on in order to have enough time to cover the next topic.

Students are enriched when they receive periodic feedback about their progress with challenging activities. Teachers who don't check for prior knowledge don't know if the planned activities will be challenging. Students who plod along through class with no idea how they're doing aren't likely to adjust along the way when headed in the wrong direction. One of the best ways to address this issue is through the use of varied assessment techniques.

Teachers often *plan* for higher levels of learning, but *assess* lower levels, such as knowledge and comprehension. The actions set out in Figure 2.1 (p. 34) should be present in planning, instruction, and assessment. The practice of calling on the first hand that goes up raises the concern that if a student is able to respond immediately, then thinking was not required, only recall. In addition, how does calling on the first person challenge the rest of the class? Many students don't respond because the same one or two students will do it for them, and if not, then the teacher will answer the question herself.

Assessments must challenge students to go beyond the who, what, and where. Teachers should pose questions to the class that require thinking, which requires time to process: "Think about how you would resolve this conflict if you were the president of the company. We will list your ideas on the board after you have had time to reach a conclusion." "If you have already determined why the chemicals reacted the way they did, predict what would happen if we lowered the temperature." Changing the conditions is an excellent way for students to be challenged while increasing the likelihood for transfer.

Processing and Reflection

Journal writing exercises can help students reflect after new information is presented. ("We have just watched a video clip of Pearl Harbor. Take out your journals, and write a short paragraph describing how you feel after seeing what happened.") Alternatively, students can satisfy their need to talk by reflecting along with their neighbors. "As your partner shows a word on the flash card, tell him what that word means to you. Then switch roles." The effective teacher realizes that students are social beings and structures time during the class period for them to talk to their classmates in a meaningful manner.

The amount of time needed for reflection depends on the difficulty of the material and the skills of the student. As Jensen (1998) wrote, "Teaching 'heavy, new' content to novice learners may require a processing time of 2–5 minutes every 10–15 minutes. But a review of old-hat material to well-rehearsed learners may require only a minute or so every 20 minutes" (p. 47).

A critical ingredient for the successful completion of processing time is choice. Students process in different ways depending on their learning styles and personal preferences. Some may want to draw pictures that capture essential information; others may prefer to create an outline, table, or chart that helps them organize the important details.

Motivation

The amount of attention that students give to a situation depends heavily on their motivation at the time of the event. Teachers can greatly affect motivation by removing threats, reducing stress, providing positive feedback, and introducing novelty. Threats can come from outside of school, from other students, or from teachers. The easiest of these to control is threat from the teacher, who should phrase any discussion of consequences in a nonthreatening manner. Rather than say, "If you don't have your homework tomorrow, you will get a zero," the teacher could say, "Having your homework done will help you bring up your grade." Rather than, "If you continue to talk, you will have detention after school," the teacher could say, "I need your full attention so that you will be prepared to complete the lab successfully. The directions will not be repeated."

Problems can best be corrected by determining what causes them to occur. Students are often off task because they don't see the urgency in completing what was assigned to them. When an activity runs short and time is left at the end of the class period, few students will start their homework as directed or study for the test to be held at the end of the week. The end of the period is a great time for practice or reflection, but this must be planned for ahead of time.

Emotion

Teachers can either make emotion work for them or allow emotion to get in the way of learning. To make emotions work positively, teachers need to have strategies for determining how students feel from time to time. Finding out about students' lives outside the classroom can give teachers valuable information about why students act the way they do. Rather than asking students, "What did you do this summer?" teachers should instruct them to write about the things that make them sad or happy. When students pick the topic of the journal entries, teachers can learn information regarding what emotions will be affecting their performance that day.

Discussing students' feelings with them also shows that teachers care about them as individuals. As the saying goes, "They don't care how much you know until they know how much you care." Teachers should also share their own emotions with students when appropriate, and they should model a love for learning and accomplishment.

Sometimes, it helps to set up activities that will bring about conflicting emotions—students need to develop strategies for dealing with their feelings and the feelings of others in a positive manner. "Research indicates that when emotions are engaged right after a learning experience, the memories are much more likely to be recalled and accuracy goes up" (McGaugh et al., in Jensen, 1998, p. 80).

Feedback can greatly affect emotions and subsequently motivation. Students who always hear "no" after attempting to answer a question are unlikely to continue to respond. Writing assignments covered with negative comments lead students to question if the effort is worth it. Teachers who award no credit unless the answer is entirely correct elicit different emotions than do those who give partial credit. Giving partial credit acknowledges the student's attempt and increases the likelihood of continued effort on his part.

Meaning

Teachers can increase the probability that students will draw connections to material by providing choice whenever possible. For instance, a student who dislikes reading novels may prefer to read extensively about skateboards; it's often not the act of reading that students dislike but rather the topic. This doesn't mean that students should be exposed only to topics that interest them, but that a mixture of what they want and what they need can produce positive results. The use of current events, family trees, and personal narratives in lessons helps make learning meaningful for students.

Student-to-student conversation is too often discouraged rather than encouraged using certain guidelines. Meaning is added when students talk together to share stories or react to information that has been presented by the teacher. Often, students can help each other learn new information because they share the same perspective. Teachers should never assume that students are using the same lenses that they are using.

Memory

Mnemonic devices are effective memory tools for many students. Using ROY G BIV for the primary and secondary colors, Every Good Boy Does Fine for the lines of the treble staff in music, PEMDAS for the order of operations, and the FOIL method for multiplying two expressions are all ways to facilitate retrieval of information.

Two of the most important times in a class period are the beginning and the end. Having students provide closure at the end of class is a great way to check their understanding and to increase their chances of remembering that information the next day. During instruction, it's important for teachers to stop periodically and have students reflect on or practice what they have learned. It's not effective to have one student or the teacher provide the answer. Instead, all students should be engaged in activities that cause them to reflect on and internalize what they have experienced.

Specific Learning Strategies

Many of the conditions needed for learning overlap. Memory improves when the information is meaningful; emotions affect attention. The important thing is that teachers practice strategies that improve learning and discard those that inhibit it. All strategies should be judged by how they affect learning.

The remainder of this chapter focuses on specific learning strategies that Marzano, Pickering, and Pollock (2001) have found to have positive effects on student learning. For each of the strategies listed below, I share some thoughts based on my observations of their use in classrooms.

Cooperative Learning

Cooperative learning is a popular teaching strategy used in schools today. According to Johnson and Johnson (1984), there are five major elements of cooperative learning:

- Positive interdependence (students rely on each other for accomplishment of the goal)
- Face-to-face promotive interaction (peers provide feedback and acknowledge success)
- Individual and group accountability (each member of the group, as well as the whole group, receives feedback)
- Interpersonal and small group skills (communication, trust, leadership, decision making, and conflict resolution)
- Group processing (evaluating how well the group is doing and what needs to be done to improve)

These elements distinguish cooperative learning from what is merely group work. It's important to make this distinction because the benefits of cooperative learning are not achieved merely by putting students in groups. If five students get together and each takes 5 of 25 questions to work on and then copy from each other, they aren't engaging in cooperative learning. Designing effective cooperative learning is hard work that can't be accomplished successfully in a few class periods. Some teachers don't use this technique because they had an unsuccessful experience that may have resulted in a loss of class control. It's not uncommon to hear, "I tried that cooperative learning thing a few times, but it didn't work."

Prior planning can greatly increase the likelihood of success when using cooperative learning. Certain decisions need to be made; for example, how should students be assigned to groups? Great care should be taken when forming groups on the basis of ability. The research is clear that continually putting struggling students in the same group is detrimental, whereas placing advanced students together has little to no effect (Marzano, Pickering, & Pollock, 2001).

The key is variety. Some days, the grouping can be random. For some activities, the grouping may be based on interests; for example, students who like sports could research a certain time period in history class and another group could be made up of students who share a love of music. In some situations, students could be assigned according to their special talents. Some students like to lead, some like to record, and some are good facilitators, so finding the best fit often determines the success of the group.

The size of the group should routinely be small. If all students are expected to participate, groups of five or more students will have a hard time meeting the five criteria for cooperative learning described earlier. Groups usually work best when they consist of three to four students (Kagan, 1994). For short periods of time, groups of two can be highly effective. Students should be grouped often enough that they remember how to function in a group.

The following basic guidelines can help teachers make cooperative learning more effective:

If it doesn't fit, don't wear it. Setting up the desks in quads with four students facing each other is a good way to get students ready for sharing. However, if the source of information is the teacher at the front of the classroom or a map on the side wall, this configuration may make it difficult to get and keep the students' attention—if you don't have the students' eyes, you don't have their ears. Change the seating arrangement to best facilitate the accomplishment of the objective. Sometimes, pushing all of the seats to the wall and leaving a big common area in the middle might work best. Having the students sit in quads all year is no more of a novelty than having them sit in rows.

Set up the process before worrying about content. Students should be aware of the process expected during cooperative learning. Setting up specific guidelines early allows the teacher to help with content as the routine becomes established. Students should be able to ask questions of the teacher only if no one in their group knows the answer. Students should all contribute using "group voices" that are quieter than individual response voices. In addition, students should decide upon roles. Who will keep the group on track? Who will record? Who will get supplies? Who will make sure that all members contribute?

Don't "bumblebee." It's common to see a teacher jump from group to group the minute the task is assigned. Sometimes, she repeats directions—which only encourages students not to listen the first time. Sometimes, her need to teach overpowers her need to have the students learn; she doesn't trust that they can actually get it on their own, so she's hesitant to relinquish her power to them. During the first few days (sometimes weeks) of using cooperative learning, the teacher should sit back and observe the process. Who works well together? Who is observing the guidelines? What strengths are evident among the groups? Once the process becomes routine, it should need only sporadic attention. This will allow the teacher to move about without being pulled in various directions by the students. She can clarify information to help students who are lost.

Identifying Similarities and Differences

The use of various techniques to identify similarities and differences is not new. Examples include the use of Venn diagrams in mathematics, classification systems in science, and analogies and metaphors in English. What is different is that these techniques are now being used successfully in other subjects. For example, teacher Debi Stover had her students use two large plastic rings in her civics class to compare and contrast the powers of the federal and state governments. Sitting on the floor in the hallway, the students worked with partners to place in piles small cards with powers listed on them: one for powers belonging specifically to the state government, one for powers belonging to the federal government, and one for powers shared by both. She was impressed with how much this helped the students retain the information compared with traditional methods of delivery. This technique can be applied to a variety of subjects.

Summarizing, Note Taking, and Interactive Notebooks

As more and more information is readily available for students, summarizing and note taking become essential skills. Students must be able to ignore irrelevant information and select or retain only the material that's important for understanding the main idea.

Another important asset is the ability to piece together the meaningful information so that the big picture becomes evident, rather than having only a collection of unrelated facts, which will not be retained. Assessing for learning requires the teacher to provide thought-provoking questions to get the students to synthesize, evaluate, and/or apply the information they have gathered (see Chapter 4).

One of the greatest wastes of student time and effort is copying notes. Some teachers read from their own notes so that students can record what they hear on paper. Others put the notes on the board or an overhead, or ask students to copy from the textbook. In some cases, cloze notes are provided that offer the bulk of the notes but require students to fill in information as it's presented. A popular trend is for teachers to put the notes in a PowerPoint presentation that the students then copy. This process often becomes no more than an electronic lecture. All of these techniques operate according to the premise that there's a fixed amount of information that students must put on paper and memorize. One excuse that I have heard in support of this technique is that it prepares the students for college. In my opinion, the best way to prepare students for college or life after high school is to have them think.

I have seen much improvement in note taking when teachers use a technique called *interactive notebooks* (INB). This often involves the teacher giving copies of the essential notes to students to paste in their binders. Across from the pages with the notes, the students use pictures, charts, or symbols to help them understand and remember the material that was pasted. In so doing, the students construct meaning for themselves rather than merely repeat how someone else interpreted the information.

Debi Stover has students fill in frames while taking notes (see Figure 3.1). By doing this, students relay the information in their own words but in an organized manner. This process helps them collect the most important information that's presented.

Homework and Practice

The practice of assigning homework is common in most schools, but varies widely. Some teachers assign homework every night, whereas others hardly ever do. Some homework is graded, some is merely checked for effort, and some is ignored. Despite these differences, some common characteristics should be present if the assignment of homework is to be worthwhile:

- Homework should be an extension of what happens in the classroom and not a "drill and kill" exercise in which students merely repeat the same skills over and over that they performed in class.
- There must be some form of urgency attached to the completion of homework. If the reward for students who complete

FIGURE 3.1
Frame for SOL 3c

Key Topic: Duties Things Citizens Are Required to Do by Law			
Main Idea	**Main Idea**	**Main Idea**	**Main Idea**
Obey laws	Pay taxes	Serve military	Serve court
Essential Details	**Essential Details**	**Essential Details**	**Essential Details**
Keep order	Sales tax	If called	If called
Keep from hurting others	Income tax	18-yr-old males register	Jury duty
Protect citizen rights	Pay for education, roads, and defense	Protect national peace	Witness
		Protect nation's security	
So what? What is important to understand about this?			
For the government to be effective, citizens must do their duties or face legal consequences.			

homework is the same as for those who don't, teachers can't expect students to expend much effort in the future. This doesn't mean that homework has to be graded. Students can be responsible for sharing with their teams or reporting to the class. Peer pressure can be very motivating without the teacher's getting caught in a paper blizzard.

- The assignment of homework should take advantage of resources that aren't available in the school setting. For example, "Ask your grandparents . . . ," or "As you watch commercials tonight . . . ," or "While you are at work after school . . ."

- Homework is what is done outside of school. Teachers should resist the temptation to let students start homework if time allows during class time. There's nothing wrong with students working sample problems followed by feedback, but that shouldn't take the place of homework.

- Homework should be graded with care. The playing field at home is not level for all students: Whereas some have access to vast resources at home, including educated and dedicated parents, computers, and materials, others might have to work until late in the night or go home to abusive or neglectful parents. Many students are responsible for babysitting their siblings. Helping students after school is one way to level the playing field.

Nonlinguistic Representations

Students are engaged in nonlinguistic representations when they gather information in ways other than hearing about it or reading about it: They make models of it, draw it, use manipulatives to touch it, organize it graphically so that spatial relationships can be noted, or act it out. Some examples of graphic organizers can be found at www.sdcoe.k12.ca.us/score/actbank/torganiz.htm.

Kinesthetic learners react positively to movement. Tactile learners relate to things they can touch. Of the eight intelligences that Gardner (1983) describes, only one relates directly to linguistics. Unfortunately, teachers typically dispense information through linguistic representation. Why? Because the focus is on teaching, not on learning, and that's how teachers were taught. However, using INBs, as described earlier in this chapter, is an excellent way to engage multiple senses so that the students take ownership of the information rather than just "rent" it until after the test.

Reinforcing Effort and Providing Recognition

It's unfortunate that many of our practices in schools discourage, rather than encourage, students' efforts. The student who raises his hand to answer a question and gets "no" as the response from the teacher quickly decides not to bother. The effective teacher dignifies the student's response by finding something to support his effort:

"You are on the right track, but I need a little more information. Can someone help?"

Teachers also discourage effort when they post a zero on an assignment because the final answer was wrong or the format was not what was desired. That same teacher later will complain about how some of the students are "unmotivated." Recognition for students who make A and A/B honor rolls is common, but how often do we recognize students who bring their grades up from an F to a C?

Setting Objectives and Providing Feedback

Marzano, Pickering, and Pollock (2001) point out that goal setting is important not only for the teacher but also for the students. Once the teacher has communicated the class's learning goals, the students should develop their own personal goals. I have found that students often have very vague goals, if any at all. If they do have goals, they typically don't have a plan to accomplish those goals from day to day. A student might say he wants a B in a given class and yet continue not to do his homework. Contracts that the teacher and the student develop collaboratively can help with this process. However, a critical component of any plan is that the student should receive frequent feedback regarding his progress toward his goal.

In some cases, the problem is not *what* we recognize but *how* we recognize. Students often get papers back with a letter grade and not much else. It's not helpful to say, "This is not your best work" or "You need to study more for tests." The feedback needs to be specific and have the goal of providing information that will help the student improve. Students can't monitor their learning in the absence of specific feedback, which must have the purpose of improving performance by identifying strengths and weaknesses in the work. It is the product, not the person who produced it, that should be evaluated.

Generating and Testing Hypotheses

One of the best ways to have students pull information together and understand the big picture is through generating and testing hypotheses. A powerful strategy is to have students stop after reading a few chapters in a novel and predict what will happen next. After finding out the answer, they can analyze the process they used to arrive at their conclusions, regardless of whether or not they were accurate. When we examine learning, the process used is often as important as the result.

Problem solving, historical investigation, invention, experimental inquiry, and decision making are all techniques that use the generating and testing of hypotheses (Marzano et al., 2001). These techniques can be used in isolation or in various combinations. The key to their success is to get students to think and use a process that works for them. This approach is consistent with the constructivist view to learning. Students also can benefit from hearing about a variety of methods used by other students to reach their conclusions. Having a procedure for gathering and interpreting facts in order to reach hypotheses will promote transfer to other situations.

Cues, Questions, and Advance Organizers

The purpose of using cues, questions, and advance organizers is to activate prior knowledge and check for understanding. Asking a question prior to instruction serves to prepare students for the lesson of the day and to determine if they possess the necessary skills to move forward. The level of the questioning (Bloom's taxonomy) should vary depending on the objective. After the question is asked, wait time should be provided to allow for deep thought and to give all students an equal chance to respond. Providing a cue following an incorrect response can turn a negative experience into a positive one for the student and increase the likelihood of future participation. (Questioning is described in detail in Chapter 4.)

Advance organizers—that is, graphic organizers used in advance of a lesson—can help students pull together the information they already have in a meaningful manner prior to new learning. Marzano and colleagues (2001) list four types of advance organizers: expository, narrative, skimming, and illustrated. Using advance organizers can greatly increase students' success in future experiences. Success can give them confidence by letting them see how much they already know before the start of instruction.

Differentiated Instruction

Teaching for learning and differentiated instruction go hand in hand. When a teacher decides to use differentiated instruction, she makes a commitment to have all students learn. The focus is on student learning, not on teaching. The starting point is to assess the learning style, readiness, and interest of each student. Using this information, the teacher adjusts the process, content, or product to meet the needs of each student. She looks at each student's strengths, not at his weaknesses. She doesn't ask how she can motivate her students; she asks how she can take advantage of what motivates them to increase their learning. The student doesn't have to fit into the agenda; rather, the agenda is adjusted to fit the student.

What's the Point?

- Teaching should be guided by what we know about how the brain learns.
- Many traditional practices inhibit learning.
- Many high-yield instructional strategies are available that can promote learning.

4

Assessing for Learning

Essential Question: How can assessment help students learn?

In this chapter, I discuss information that encourages teachers to assess for learning. According to Black and William (1998), formative assessment is at the heart of teaching. They note that "teaching and learning must be interactive," and that "assessment becomes formative assessment when the evidence is actually used to adapt the teaching to meet student needs" (p. 2). They also point to studies showing "that innovations that include strengthening the practice of formative assessment produce significant and often substantial learning gains. Many of these studies arrive at another important conclusion: that improved formative assessment helps low achievers more than other students and therefore reduces the range of achievement while raising achievement overall" (p. 3).

Black and William note that formative assessment

- "Involves new ways to enhance feedback between those taught and the teacher, ways that will require significant changes in classroom practice,"
- Assumes "that students have to be actively involved" in learning, and

- Yields results "that have to be used to adjust teaching and learning," so that "a significant aspect of any program will be the ways in which teachers make these adjustments." (p. 2)

Stiggins (2002) suggests that formative assessment and assessment for learning aren't the same: "Assessment for learning is about far more than testing more frequently or providing teachers with evidence so that they can revise instruction, although these steps are part of it. In addition, we now understand that assessment for learning must involve students in the process" (p. 5).

Some of my teachers expressed confusion regarding the difference between assessment *for* learning and assessment *of* learning. I used Figure 4.1 to show them the differences as I saw them.

FIGURE 4.1

Comparison of Assessment *for* Learning and Assessment *of* Learning

Assessment *for* Learning	Assessment *of* Learning
Formative	Summative
Asks what is happening	Asks what happened
Involves the use of white boards, signaling, choral responses, flash cards, and so on	Involves the use of tests
"They (the students) learned it"	"We (the teachers) taught it"
Occurs before, during, and at the end of daily instruction	Occurs at the end of a major unit, quarter, or semester
Causes an immediate change in instructional strategies based on the responses from students	May guide planning for the next year
In medical terms: a regular checkup	In medical terms: an autopsy

It's unfortunate that current practices miss the mark regarding formative assessment or assessment for learning. Brooks and Brooks (1993) describe the situation as it exists in many classrooms, where they believe that "student thinking is devalued":

When asking students questions, most teachers seek not to enable students to think through intricate issues, but to discover whether students know the "right" answers. Consequently, students quickly learn not to raise their hands in response to a teacher's question unless they are confident they already know the sought-after response. Doing otherwise places them at some risk. . . . Schooling is premised on the notion that there exists a fixed world that the learner must come to know. (p. 7)

Black and William (1998) explain that teachers try to direct their students toward giving the expected answer because they lack "the flexibility or the confidence to deal with the unexpected . . . In manipulating the dialogue in this way, the teacher seals off any unusual, often thoughtful but unorthodox attempts by pupils to work out their own answers. Over time the pupils get the message: They are not required to think out their own answers. The object of the exercise is to work out—or guess—what answer the teacher expects to see or hear" (p. 7). Because the goal is to have someone supply the correct answer, questions that involve higher levels of understanding are replaced by low-level checks for knowledge and comprehension. In addition, there's very little time between the delivery of the question and the expected response. Although many studies have documented the importance of increasing wait time (Rowe, 1972), little has changed in the classroom. Teachers don't wait before moving from one student to another. In some classrooms, waiting becomes a control issue: Advanced students call out the answer rather than wait for students who need more time to respond. Many teachers tell students to raise their hands to answer a question, but respond to the first student who calls out.

Another problem is that the same students typically answer the questions. Sometimes, they initiate the response by calling out or raising their hands; other times, the teacher calls on them. Either way, the distribution of teacher/student interaction is very unbalanced in most classrooms. This uneven distribution sets up competition rather than collaboration among students. Advanced students get their hands up almost before the teacher finishes posing the question; they wave their hands high in the air, seeking acknowledgment. Slower students sit passively, waiting for a classmate or the teacher to supply the "correct" response. In order to avoid the risk of sounding stupid, these students choose not to answer at all (Black & William, 1998).

In this situation that Brooks and Brooks (1993) describe, the teacher obviously is trying to get many students involved:

> We have all been in classrooms where the teacher poses a question to the students and hands shoot up excitedly. The teacher then peers about the room and calls on a student. The student answers, and the teacher says, "No." The teacher then calls on a second student. That student answers, and the teacher, shaking his head from side to side, says, "Uh-uh." The teacher then calls upon a third student, and as she answers, the teacher says, "Close, but not quite." A fourth intrepid student raises his hand. Upon answering, the teacher shakes his head affirmatively and says, "Yes, THAT'S the right answer!" (p. 85)

There are many problems with this method of questioning. How do the students feel who don't guess what's on the teacher's mind? Neuroscience has revealed that students who feel threatened aren't able to learn as well as when they are in a safe environment (Jensen, 1998). Calling on a student to answer a question in front of his peers can be threatening. This is especially true when there's little time for the student to process the question. He's on the spot the minute his name is mentioned. Students often raise their hands to answer the first question, but freeze when a follow-up question is posed. They don't plan on having to provide details, so the second question produces stress, which in turn causes them to give up or provide an incorrect answer. After another student raises her hand to answer the follow-up question, the first student often realizes that he could have responded successfully if he'd had time to process the question without the threat of embarrassment.

Some students participate freely in one class but sit quietly in others. This is often due to their levels of comfort, not just with the subject matter but also with the rewards or risks associated with participation. Most students who don't participate in class often question their abilities. It doesn't take very long for them to realize that effort doesn't replace lack of ability: When they make an effort, they're not rewarded if the teacher says "no" and moves on to someone else. However, some students don't participate for the opposite reason: If the level of difficulty is too low, advanced students often tune out. They get no thrill from answering questions that they deem beneath their level of comprehension. In fact, they often get irritated with the teacher who calls on students who aren't able to answer the questions. This seems like a waste of time to some advanced students.

Another factor that determines whether students respond to questions is their level of interest. If students don't perceive the topic to be meaningful or relevant to them, they coast along hoping that the time spent on it will be minimal. It's not uncommon for advanced students to provide inaccurate responses to relatively simple questions. It's not that they don't know the answers; it's that they don't care. As I sit in the back of classrooms, I frequently hear students whisper correct responses that they keep to themselves rather than share with the class. They quickly learn that the reward for answering is not as great as the risk.

The method of questioning not only affects how students feel but what and how they learn. What's the effect on students when they hear three incorrect answers before they hear one that's correct? A silly response from one student, which causes the students to laugh, may register in their brains much longer than the correct response will. The emotion that is attached to the event causes longer retention. Likewise, if the student gives a "stupid" answer when called upon, he may later block that out of his memory along with the correct answer that was provided by the teacher or another student.

Hunter (1982) suggests that teachers often commit three common errors: "The first error is to assume, because students are quiet or nod their heads up and down, that they understand. A second error is to say, 'You all understand, don't you?' This question implies that students who do not understand either were not paying attention or they are not very intelligent. A third error is to ask the class if anyone has a question. . . . All three of these dysfunctional methods for checking student understanding can result in a teacher's proceeding, blissfully unaware that students are lost." Although determining which students don't understand is one of the most important things a teacher can do, it's also one of the hardest. Students will rarely volunteer an inability to comprehend.

After witnessing teachers using some of the techniques I have just described, I have heard the following responses from students:

- "Why should I raise my hand? If the smart kids don't answer the question right away, the teacher will call on them or answer the question herself."
- "I can't think as fast as the students who answer the questions."
- "I don't want the rest of the class to know that I'm stupid."
- "If I don't answer when called on, the teacher will go on to someone else. That's better than saying something dumb in front of everyone."
- "It doesn't matter how hard I try, I still fail."
- "I get really nervous and can't think when she calls on me."

Often, the same students hear "no" when they respond to questions period after period, day after day, year after year. They develop a pattern of not participating rather than risking embarrassment. Telling the teacher (and the class) that they didn't bring their textbook is not as painful as letting everyone know that they can't read. It's less embarrassing for students to have no completed homework to turn in than to bring in only the little that they know how to complete successfully.

In some situations, it's good to call on individual students. When brainstorming is the goal, students can call out in a rapid-fire manner or raise their hands to be called on. In these examples, there are often multiple answers and divergent thinking is applauded: "In what ways are trees different from cars?" "Tell me everything you know about lightbulbs." "What does the word *compassion* mean to you?" Wait time is not necessary, and the focus is more on quantity than on quality.

When individuals are called upon, teachers should use certain techniques to make the experience positive. Most teachers are good at providing positive reinforcement following a correct response. However, what they do following a partial or incorrect response may be more important. Hunter (1982) points out that the teacher should always dignify student responses. This is accomplished by accepting the response and pointing out what is correct: "That would have been correct if I asked you to list a job of the president, but I was looking for a job of the vice president." Quite often, the student can be successful with a little help. Rephrasing the question often helps, as does cueing: "Remember what happened when we did the experiment yesterday?" "Think about what we said about characteristics of living things." Leaving a student for a moment may take some of the pressure off and give her time to think. If she still doesn't have the answer, ask someone to help her and then ask her if what her classmate said makes sense. Whatever technique is used, the student must feel that there was some reward for her efforts. I have heard some teachers say, "OK, I see where you're coming from," even when the answer is from left field. Others have said, "Thanks for sharing. Who can add to that?"

It's also important to probe after a correct response. All students can be challenged to think at higher levels when prodded by follow-up questions: "You are correct in that situation, but what if the amount of time available was not a factor?" "How does that apply to the current crisis overseas?" "Why is it important for us to know that information?" However, as Hunter (1982) points out, there are problems with relying on individual responses. The biggest problem is assuming that the other students "have it" because one student gets it right; the solution can be as simple as replacing "Does anyone know?" with "How many of you know?"

The level of questioning should be varied and balanced, and should combine knowledge/comprehension questions with some application, synthesis, and evaluation questions. Higher-level questioning must be accompanied by increased wait time. The goal should be to have students think, not merely respond. After a sufficient period of time, students should raise their hands to signify that they have an answer to the question (not simply that they want to respond). Having only a few hands go up should be a red flag that students either don't understand the question or don't know the answer. If a significant number of hands go up, the teacher may choose to have the students share what their partners have said. Having students discuss their answers with partners prior to sharing with the class increases their confidence level and probability of success.

Group Checking for Understanding

Group checking for understanding provides valuable information for the teacher and increases student engagement. There are many ways that teachers can perform group checking for understanding. The methods can be whatever the teacher is comfortable with; they can change during the class period or be based on the type of information needed. The key to success is that the characteristics listed below be present:

- Information is gathered from all students.
- The response provides information regarding the level of mastery of the objective.
- Participation is nonthreatening.
- The results guide decisions regarding future instruction.
- Students receive feedback for self-assessment.
- Information can be gathered and processed quickly.
- Feedback is specific.

Techniques

The following techniques meet the criteria for conducting efficient group checks for understanding.

Hand signaling. Students can give thumbs up if they understand or agree with what the teacher has said, thumbs down if they don't, or a wave motion with their hands if they're not sure. Similarly, the students can provide hand signals for the numbers one, two, or three to signify which category they select from those listed on the board. (For example, the teacher could call out words and have the students signal if the word is a [1] noun, [2] verb, or [3] adjective.) If students look around to see how others are signaling, the teacher knows that they aren't sure of their answers. Time should be provided after the word is called out so that all students have time to think about their responses. Some teachers have students close their eyes during this exercise to eliminate distractions.

Choral responses. Rather than calling on individuals, teachers can solicit choral responses from the class. This practice is most common in foreign language classes. It's not as accurate as some of the others, but it can be effective if used properly. Teachers should vary the strategy so that the same small group doesn't provide all the answers. Calling on rows or tables can reduce this problem. The main benefits of this strategy are that the pressure is off the individual and that more students practice at any one given time.

Exit cards. Students can use notecards to list what they learned that day, what confused them, or what they want to know more about. They can give the cards to the teacher as they leave.

Flash cards. One card can be given to each student, with an A and an upside-down B on one side and a C and an upside-down D on the other side. Students then listen to multiple-choice questions or see them on a monitor as the teacher uses PowerPoint or some other presentation device. On command, students merely display their answers.

Partners. A variation of the hand-signaling technique involves using partners. Prior to answering, the students could check with their partners. When asked to signal, students could provide their partner's response rather than their own. This reduces pressure and encourages students to work together and communicate their thoughts. I have seen teachers pose a question to the class and get two or three hands in the air. The teacher tells the students to check with their partners. When she repeats the question, the number of hands up usually increases significantly. By checking with their partners, students gain confidence that their participation won't result in embarrassment.

Sequence strips. These are useful when teachers want students to place certain information in the proper order. A baggie containing certain words or phrases can be provided to students, who then put the information in the correct order on their desks for the teacher to see. A variation of this is to put pieces of a puzzle in the baggie for students to put together to form various shapes: "Use the puzzle pieces to make five pizzas containing examples of the five types of plants we discussed."

Whiteboards. Teachers can pose a problem to the class, and when prompted, the students can write their answers on the whiteboard. In mathematics classes, teachers can see how the students worked the problem rather than just hear their answers. Students typically like this variation to paper and pencil. Commercial whiteboards, dry erase markers, and erasers can be purchased in a set. Some shops sell single four- by eight-foot sheets of "shower board" that can be divided into 32 one-foot-square boards for individual student use. Dry erase markers can be added to students' list of supplies to be purchased by parents at the beginning of the year. A box of tissues or sheets of washable felt work very nicely in the place of erasers.

The above strategies must be performed on a regular basis so that students are aware of the procedures and they become part of the daily routine. Strategies should be used before, during, and near the conclusion of the class period. Using a variety of techniques can increase motivation and attention.

The following two scenarios illustrate how group checking for understanding can engage more students and give the teacher more accurate feedback regarding their progress. A mathematics teacher who focuses on *teaching* might begin her check of homework as follows:

> She asks, "Which problem from last night's homework do you want me to work?" She then provides the process, and calls on the students one by one to carry out the operations. Or she may ask four students to go to the board and work problems 1 through 4, then have four different students work questions 5 through 8, and so on. When the students are done, the teacher asks, "Does everyone understand?" Students typically don't respond if they still don't understand.

Whether the teacher or the students work the problems, the conditions are the same: The same attention is given to the problems that most students got correct as to the problems that all might have missed. The teacher does most of the work while students watch. What becomes evident from this exercise is that the teacher knows how to do the homework.

When the teacher's emphasis is on *learning*, she might conduct the group check this way:

> "I have put the 20 answers to last night's homework on the overhead. Give me a quick thumbs up or down to let me know how you did on each problem. Number one? Good! Number two? Super! Number three? Wow, that one gave you some

trouble. Number four?" And so on. Then, "OK, we need to find out what happened with number three. Share what you did with your partner. Did you and your partner find out you made a process error or a mechanical error? Here are three more problems similar to number three. Work these problems, and then discuss them with your partner while I walk around to help."

In this scenario, the teacher diagnoses the area needing attention and provides the students with input and practice where it's most needed. The emphasis is on what the students need to learn, not merely on what the teacher wants to cover.

Black and William (1998) suggest that how teachers teach and check for understanding depends on whether they think students have a fixed IQ or have untapped potential. They add that "teachers need . . . a variety of living examples of implementation, as practiced by teachers with whom they can identify and from whom they can derive the confidence that they can do better" (p. 8). Figure 4.2 could be a starting point for teachers to see examples from various disciplines. They should be encouraged to build a similar chart for their disciplines by working year after year with teachers in their subject areas.

Self-Reflection

There are three main reasons for using assessment for learning. I discussed the first two earlier in this chapter: (1) To guide teacher decision making during the class period and (2) to help students to think and practice. The third reason is to increase student motivation through self-reflection.

I love to play golf. My skills are good enough that I can play with most Sunday golfers without embarrassing myself. Some of my most enjoyable days on the course are when I don't use a scorecard. This allows me to remember the great shots and the holes where I made par but to forget the shots that were out of bounds and double

FIGURE 4.2
Checking for Understanding

To Show That They Learned . . .	The Students . . .
The meaning of the vocabulary words	Labeled the dependent variable, independent variable, constant, and control in four different scenarios as the teacher walked around the room.
How to identify pronouns	Gave thumbs up when a pronoun was used in the song they were listening to.
How to divide fractions	Showed the steps and answers to five problems on their white boards.
The four main causes of the Civil War	Raised their hands to signal that their partners could list them without help.
The steps for solving word problems	Placed the labeled strips in the correct order on their desks.
Certain vocabulary words in Spanish	Gave choral responses as pieces of fruit were held up by the teacher.

bogies. It's unfortunate that someone in my group often keeps score without my knowledge. When the scores are totaled at the end of the round, the 85 I thought I had turns into a 92.

When I talk to students about their current standings in class, their replies often resemble my "assumed" golf score. They remember the good grades but forget the test they bombed or the project they didn't turn in. It's this escape from reality that allows them to glide through the marking period feeling that all is well, and that results in disappointment when the report card comes out. Students often feel that their attendance in class, rather than their effort, will determine their progress.

The student who has no idea where he is, or where he needs to be, will see no need to change his behavior. Classroom assessment that involves students in the process and focuses on increasing learn-ing can motivate rather than merely measure students (Chappuis & Stiggins, 2002). Students involved in their own assessment might do the following:

- Determine the attributes of good performance.
- Use scoring guides to evaluate real-world samples.
- Revise anonymous work samples.
- Create practice tests or test items based on their understand-ing of the learning targets and the essential concepts.
- Communicate with others about their growth, and determine when they are nearing success. (Chappuis & Stiggins, 2002)

Peer editing is an effective way to have students produce qual-ity work. The author of the work receives feedback from someone her own age (an "editor") who "speaks her language," and the editor gains a better understanding of her own work by using a rubric to provide feedback for someone else.

Regardless of the method of feedback used, the emphasis of assessment must be on progress, not just on perfection. If a student sees that his scores improve by 10 points from one test to another, he might be motivated to try harder. Students should leave class each day with an understanding of what they gained rather than of how they fell further behind.

Learning Logs

Teacher Lynda Fairman has her students complete *learning logs*. These are brief statements about what they learned in each class every day. Reflection of this type can boost students' confidence as they prepare for future assessments. It's also good for parents who otherwise might get a response of "nothing" from their child when inquiring as to what happened in school that day. The following is an example of a learning log:

Today in Chorus, I learned that posture is important in singing.
Today in Civics, I learned that there are three branches of government and that they check on each other.
Today in Math, I learned that showing your work can help you eliminate mistakes.
Today in Gym, I learned that follow-through is very important when attempting a foul shot.
Today in Art, I learned that shading can make a picture look lifelike.
Today in English, I learned that rap lyrics are a form of poetry.
Today in Science, I learned the difference between an independent variable and dependent variable, I think.

In all cases, the purpose of formative checking is *to assess learning, not to evaluate it,* in order to guide future instruction. The teacher should alter her plans when she discovers that students aren't progressing toward mastery of the objective. This alteration should be based on the results of checking the whole class, not merely a few students.

In order to help teachers focus on learning rather than teaching, those who train and provide feedback for teachers need to have the same focus. The rest of this book provides a framework for that to occur.

What's the Point?

- Traditional methods of assessing student progress verify what the teacher has taught by having one student respond at a time.
- Assessment for learning verifies what all students have learned and are learning in order to guide subsequent activities.
- Many techniques are available that let the teacher and the student know how well the student is mastering the objective.

- Any technique should include a variety of learning levels (from Bloom's taxonomy, for example). Students should be required to think and demonstrate deep understanding, not just to recall what they have memorized.

5

Learner Observations

Essential Question: What is the best way for an observer to gather important information while performing a classroom observation?

The first four chapters of this book present a rationale for teachers to focus on learning, not just on teaching. Some of the ideas presented were relatively new; others have been around for a long time. However, little has changed over the past 100 years in the way we teach. The problem is not that teachers are not exposed to new ideas. The problem is that many teachers see no reason to change. They try something new at the beginning of the year or after returning from a conference, but the innovation doesn't last long. When new strategies start to present some challenges, they revert to their former ways. Veteran teachers often live by the motto "This too shall pass," or "The pendulum swings, wide tie, narrow tie." Many believe that there's no reason to change because today's innovation will be replaced by another hot one in the near future.

The rest of this book shares what principals can do to cause sustained improvement in their schools. In this chapter you will find various methods of performing classroom observations, as well as a discussion of whole-period observations and the five- to fifteen-minute walk-through that's popular today.

Teacher-observation procedures in schools throughout the country have many similarities. Teachers are usually informed when initial observations will take place; in some cases, pre-observation conferences are offered but rarely held. The principal or assistant principal arrives at the classroom with pad and pen ready to record the events of the day. He typically sits in the back of the room and doesn't engage in the various activities. Some observers script in a narrative form, some chart the behaviors of students and/or the teacher, some merely observe and make a few notes, and others fill in checklists.

The criteria that the observer typically looks for are dictated by the formative evaluation that's used by all administrators in the school division. Major categories typically include Planning, Delivery of Instruction, Assessment, Classroom Management, and Professional Qualities. The labels sometimes change, but the descriptors in each category are relatively the same in most schools. In most observation systems, almost all attention is given to the process used by the teacher. Did the teacher smile, use positive reinforcement, vary instructional techniques, balance interaction, use wait time?

One criterion that is absent in most formative evaluation systems is an identification of student learning. Did students master the objective? If so, how many and how well? According to Stronge, "If a student walks through a teacher's classroom 180 or 190 times, she should be better in a tangible, measurable way for the experience" (2002, p. 65). I would take this a step further to suggest that the student should gain something *every* time she walks into the classroom. And shouldn't administrators provide feedback regarding the evidence of learning that they see during an observation? Administrators typically watch the behaviors of the students in order to evaluate classroom management, yet they watch the behavior of the teacher to evaluate instruction.

The following two narratives list the various activities that another veteran administrator and I witnessed during observations.

Barry's Observation Summary

The teacher started class as soon as the bell rang. The objective and agenda for the day were clearly written on the board. An opening activity was presented that reviewed the lesson from the previous day and introduced the new lesson. A PowerPoint presentation was used to summarize key information while the teacher made connections to real-world applications. The teacher called on students during the presentation to make sure they were paying attention and that they understood what was being taught. The teacher gave positive reinforcement when students provided correct responses. When a student didn't know an answer, the teacher called on someone else or provided the information herself and then asked the first student if he understood. The teacher provided "seatwork" so the students could practice independently. As the students worked, the teacher checked on the special education students. Students who misbehaved were corrected immediately. The teacher worked a few homework problems to make sure the students understood. At the end of the lesson, the teacher provided closure by reviewing the important concepts that were taught that day.

Vicky's Observation Summary

Only three students were paying attention to the teacher when the bell rang. The other students were opening their books, asking each other for paper, or asking the teacher about directions for the activity. Students did not appear to know what the objective was, nor which activities would follow. As the teacher lectured, two students took notes, 20 students watched, and four looked around the room or out the window. When questions were asked, four students supplied the majority of the responses, 12 answered one question apiece, and 10 said they didn't know the answer when questioned. Twelve of the students completed the handout 10 minutes before the next activity. They chatted quietly as they waited for the others to finish. Six of the students stopped after attempting only half of the questions. Six of the students did not finish and appeared frustrated that they did not have enough time. Most of the students appeared to be confused when the teacher worked a homework problem. When she asked if everyone understood, they did not respond. Most students packed up their books about five minutes before the end of the period.

These two scenarios demonstrate the difference in results when the observer looks at the behavior of the teacher rather than the behaviors of the students. Although Barry and Vicky were both observing the same class at the same time, Barry watched the teacher and Vicky watched the students. Stanford and Roark (1974) note the problem with observing only the teaching processes: "Most of these attempts to humanize education have focused on content or structure and have ignored the process through which significant learning takes place, which is interaction with other human beings" (p. 5).

Research Findings on Learner Observations

Observing the behaviors of students during classroom observations is not new. The system of interaction analysis developed by Flanders (1970) during the 1960s is one of the earliest and most established methods of categorizing classroom communication. His system has 10 categories of student and teacher behaviors. Teacher behaviors include the following:

- Accepting feelings
- Praising or encouraging
- Accepting or using ideas of pupils
- Asking questions
- Lecturing
- Giving directions
- Critiquing

Student behaviors are recorded as pupil-talk-response, pupil-talk-initiation, or silence or confusion. Flanders concluded that superior achievement occurred in indirect classes (where teachers ask questions and solicit student opinions) when compared with direct classes (where teachers lecture and give directions). Indirect teachers were more alert to, more concerned with, and made greater use of statements provided by students.

In another study of teacher-pupil interaction, Brophy and Good (1970) developed the Dyadic Interaction System to determine whether teachers used different approaches with some students than with others. Dyadic interaction refers to interaction with one student about matters idiosyncratic to her. Because of individual differences among classmates, Brophy and Good conclude that the observation of dyadic teacher-pupil interaction is superior to other methods of observation, especially in assessing teacher effectiveness. As they put it, "A change in research design from the class to the individual as the unit of analysis would be more appropriate conceptually, and more powerful statistically, for evaluating the importance of these teacher behaviors" (p. 12).

Researchers have used interaction-analysis systems similar to those proposed by Flanders and Brophy and Good to make assumptions about student engagement. According to Good (1981), the behavior and the achievement of students will assimilate the expectations of the teacher. Kerman (1979) discovered that high achievers receive more response opportunities and are given more time to respond to questions. Adams and Biddle (1970) maintain that physical placement of the students in the classroom affects the extent of pupil participation: "Pupils up and down the center line of the classroom are the ones who are most likely to join in the discussion, and the ones the teacher is most likely to talk to" (p. 15).

Sadker and Sadker (1986) found that about 25 percent of elementary and secondary students typically don't interact with the teacher at all during class. In the same classes, 10 percent of the students participated in more than three times their fair share of interactions with the teacher. The Sadkers maintain that most inequity in classroom interaction is between males and females, and that this bias inhibits student achievement.

According to Edmonds (1982), "One way to discriminate between effective teachers and others is to record the proportion of students who are asked to answer questions as a function of the student's race or social class" (p. 4). Acheson and Gall (1980) developed a seating chart observation record called "At Task" that's very simple and useful for recording how students are using their time. The behaviors are charted every three minutes in the following categories: at task, stalling, other schoolwork than that requested by teacher, out of seat, and talking to neighbors.

All of these research studies share one similarity: They describe the positive relationship between student engagement and achievement. However, most of the early research treated the whole class as the unit of study, ignoring differences between individual students. Comparisons were made between various groups of students—high achievers versus low achievers, males versus females, and students seated in the front of the classroom versus students seated in other areas of the classroom. The studies that did focus on the individuals mostly recorded time on task or verbal interaction. Also, almost all of the early studies dealt with elementary students.

As Cohen (1972) notes, "We can't assume that the learning of 30 students in a classroom can be understood with the same set of ideas useful for understanding learning in a two-person tutorial situation. If the teacher explains things very well, asks questions broadly, makes students extend answers to questions, and frequently reinforces important points, it's thought that students will learn. But what if a student never raises her hand, sits in the back of the classroom, often fails to listen, and rarely engages in a question-answer interchange with her teacher? Will that student receive the same benefits as does the eager student who sits up front and has all the direct interaction with the teacher?" (p. 441).

Danielson (1996) discusses the problem with merely recording time spent on task. Her "Framework for Professional Practice" lists four domains of "what teachers should know and be able to do in the exercise of their profession" (p. 29). The third domain is devoted to instruction and includes the criterion of "Engaging students in learning." Danielson states:

> If one component can claim to be the most important, this is the one. Student engagement is not the same as "time on task," a concept that refers to student involvement in instructional activities. Students may be completing a worksheet (rather than talking or passing notes) and therefore "on task," even if the worksheet does not engage them in significant learning. Mere activity, then, is inadequate for engagement. Nor is simple participation sufficient. What is required for student engagement is intellectual involvement with the content, or active construction of understanding. School, in other words, is not a spectator sport. (p. 95)

Danielson describes the "distinguished" level of student performance as follows: "All students are cognitively engaged in the activities and assignment in their exploration of content. Students initiate or adapt activities and projects to enhance understanding" (p. 98).

Stronge (2002) also describes the need to have teachers focus on learning. He presents a "Teacher Skills Checklist" that includes five categories:

- The Teacher as a Person
- The Teacher as Classroom Manager and Organizer
- Organizing for Instruction
- Implementing Instruction
- The Teacher Teaching: Monitoring Student Progress and Potential

Each category is broken down into various qualities, which are then broken down into various indicators. Teachers are rated in each quality as follows: Not Observed, Ineffective, Apprentice, Professional, or Master. One advantage of this checklist is that teachers are encouraged to become Masters in the various categories rather than merely meet minimal expectations. Another advantage is that it's expected that the teacher will be "concerned with having students *learn and demonstrate understanding* of meaning rather than memorization" (p. 47, emphasis added).

Learner Observation System

"Learner observation" systems can be used to supplement present systems, such as those presented by Stronge and Danielson. Unlike earlier data collection systems, the goal is to have students demonstrate learning rather than merely be "on task" or interact verbally with the teacher. A modified version of this system was used at York High School in Yorktown, Virginia, from 1988 to 1999. Administrators at Tabb Middle School in Yorktown have used various versions of this system since 1999.

During a classroom observation, the observer fills in the teacher's name, the date, the number of students in the classroom, the standard of learning, and the lesson objective on a chart similar to the one in Figure 5.1. The observer typically sits in the back of the classroom so as not to disrupt instruction. However, depending on the comfort level of the students and the teacher, the observer may choose to sit in the front of the class in order to get a better view of the students. During the class period, the observer records the number of students exhibiting certain behaviors minute by minute.

The example given in Figure 5.1 has been tweaked for the purpose of describing the various components of the chart; it is not an example of a perfect lesson by any means. At 9:05 in the example provided, 12 students write the daily challenge and 12 chat. At 9:11, six students report problems with the Aristotle system. "LTT" stands for "listen to teacher." "T" is used to designate "teacher." Teacher behaviors are listed in the big box marked "Other" in each five-minute segment. In the example, "T gives wait time" is listed under the first segment.

FIGURE 5.1
Sample Learner Observation Summary

Teacher: Ima Sample   **Date:** December 7, 2005   **Number of Students:** 24   **SOL:** LS 5 a & b

The objective was for the students to be able to: Compare and contrast early classification systems with the modern classification system

Time	Qty	Description of Student Behaviors	Other			
9:05	12	Write daily challenge "What is a classification system?" 12 chat	T gives wait time			
9:06	24	Review test results from previous day				
9:07	6	Ask T questions regarding test				
9:08	12	Describe system used by Aristotle	**Wand**	**Wtch**	**Work**	**Learn**
9:09	24	Work w/ partner to classify animals using Aristotle system	10%	25%	55%	10%
9:10	24	Work w/ partner to classify animals using Aristotle system	T walks, gives help			
9:11	6	Report problems with Aristotle system				
9:12	24	LTT describe system proposed by Linnaeus				
9:13	6	Describe physical characteristic of student in front of class	**Wand**	**Wtch**	**Work**	**Learn**
9:14	6	Describe physical characteristic of student in front of class	0%	65%	30%	5%
9:15	24	Classify animal cards according to Linnaeus system w/ partner				
9:16	24	Classify animal cards according to Linnaeus system w/ partner				
9:17	6	Describe how they categorized animals				
9:18	6	LTT describe modern classification system, 18 take notes from overhead	**Wand**	**Wtch**	**Work**	**Learn**
9:19	6	LTT describe modern classification system, 18 take notes from overhead	0%	25%	70%	5%

FIGURE 5.1 (cont.)
Sample Learner Observation Summary

Time	Qty	Description of Student Behaviors	Other			
9:20	18	LTT describe evolution, 6 answer questions	Same students answer questions			
9:21	18	LTT describe evolution, 6 answer questions				
9:22	24	LTT compare cat leg, human arm				
9:23	24	LTT compare cat leg, human arm	**Wand**	**Wtch**	**Work**	**Learn**
9:24	24	LTT compare cat leg, human arm	0%	90%	10%	0%
Time	**Qty**	**Description of Student Behaviors**	**Other**			
9:25	6	Name species				
9:26	24	LTT describe embryos				
9:27	24	LTT describe modern classification system				
9:28	24	LTT describe modern classification system	**Wand**	**Wtch**	**Work**	**Learn**
9:29	24	LTT describe modern classification system	0%	95%	5%	0%
9:30	24	" " kingdom, take notes				
9:31	24	" " phylum, take notes				
9:32	24	" " class, order, family, take notes				
9:33	24	" " genus, take notes	**Wand**	**Wtch**	**Work**	**Learn**
9:34	24	" " species, take notes	0%	0%	100%	0%
9:35	24	" " levels of classification, take notes	T corrects wrong answers			
9:36	18	Practice mnemonic KPCOFGS to remember 7 levels, 6 chat				
9:37	6	Call out classification of man				
9:38	24	Put categories in order using strips	**Wand**	**Wtch**	**Work**	**Learn**
9:39	18	Pull out 2 that make up scientific name, 6 are wrong	5%	15%	60%	20%

(Figure continued on next page)

FIGURE 5.1 *(cont.)*
Sample Learner Observation Summary

Time	Qty	Description of Student Behaviors	Other			
9:40	24	Use whiteboards to show characteristics of various classification systems				
9:41	24	Use whiteboards to show characteristics of various classification systems				
9:42	24	Use whiteboards to show characteristics of various classification systems				
9:43	18	Create chart to show similarities and differences, 6 chat	**Wand**	**Wtch**	**Work**	**Learn**
9:44	18	Create chart to show similarities and differences, 6 chat	10%	0%	0%	90%
9:45	18	Create chart to show similarities and differences, 6 pack up				
9:46	18	Create chart to show similarities and differences, 6 pack up				
9:47	12	Complete exit card stating what they learned that day, 12 pack up				
9:48	12	Complete exit card stating what they learned that day, 12 pack up	**Wand**	**Wtch**	**Work**	**Learn**
9:49	12	Complete exit card stating what they learned that day, 12 pack up	60%	0%	0%	40%
		Total	10%	35%	35%	20%

During the observation, or afterwards if time does not allow, the observer fills in the percent of time during which students exhibit characteristics of the four categories (wanderers, watchers, workers, learners) listed on the right-hand side:

- *Wanderers* are students who look out the window, talk off task, or doodle.

- *Watchers* listen to a lecture, watch a movie, or observe the presentation of another student.
- *Workers* look up definitions, copy notes from the board, or answer the questions at the end of the chapter by finding the information in the textbook.
- *Learners* demonstrate the accomplishment of the objective by answering teacher questions (either as individuals or as a group), working problems at their desks that require original thought, or sharing their thoughts with their neighbors.

Figure 5.1 shows that between 9:05 and 9:09, students were wandering (chatting) 10 percent of the time, watching 25 percent of the time, working (writing daily challenges and asking questions) 55 percent of the time, and learning (describing the system used by Aristotle) 10 percent of the time. Each minute represents 20 percent of a five-minute segment. During minute 9:08, for example, half the students are observed describing Aristotle's system; that's half of 20 percent, which means that 10 percent of the students for that five-minute segment are in the learning category. Students who are not listed in a segment are usually watching.

It is important to keep in mind that *the percentages in this system are estimates*. Their purpose is to stimulate a discussion of the general behaviors of students during the class. Time should not be wasted trying to determine exact percentages. If students are watching most of the time, it doesn't matter if the percentage is 70 or 75.

At the bottom of the chart, the total is listed for each of the four categories. This number is derived by adding the percentages for each five-minute segment and then dividing by the number of segments, which in this case is nine. Again, estimates will suffice; although the total in the "wandering" category is 85, which equals 9.44 when divided by 9, the rounded average of 10 percent is recorded.

The summary in this case reveals that there was a little wandering and some evidence of learning in the class. Students were either watching or working the rest of the time. Still, caution should be used when making assumptions about data collected using this learner observation system. The purpose is to stimulate a discussion regarding teaching and learning, not to ensure a high percentage of learning. The observational chart should not be the sole criterion by which a teacher is evaluated. However, the observer can discuss the range in which an average falls: If the data show that most of the students are "watching" the majority of the time, the observer might want to suggest ways to get students overtly engaged. The absence of evidence of learning might be due to a poorly worded objective or lack of checking for group understanding.

The Walk-Through

Another means of gathering information and providing feedback for teachers involves what is commonly referred to as a *walk-through*. There are many ways to accomplish this task, but most have some characteristics in common. Typically, the walk-through is unannounced and lasts anywhere from 5 to 15 minutes. The objective is to take a quick snapshot of classroom activities followed by some type of documentation provided to the teacher. It's rare that conferences follow these visits. In some cases, observers use checklists to record specific behaviors they witness during the visit. Some observers merely jot a few notes that identify a few commendations or recommendations for the teacher.

When I send a note to a teacher following a walk-through, I choose not to list any suggestions in my feedback (see the example in Figure 5.2). My two goals are to gain information about what is occurring in the classroom and to provide the teacher with positive reinforcement. I have found it helpful to do a walk-through for teachers new to the building prior to the first announced observation. This, I hope, lowers the level of concern for the teacher because the formal observation is not the first time I see her teach. It's also useful to see if the behaviors shown during the announced observation are consistent with those observed in the walk-through. I use this procedure for the veteran teachers who I don't formally observe during the year; this allows me to acknowledge their hard work more frequently.

FIGURE 5.2
Example of Feedback Given Following a Walk-Through

Dear Mrs. Smith,

During my brief visit, I saw you using a variety of methods to check student understanding. You checked the students' prior knowledge by having them write down everything they knew about the topic during the warm-up. You had them use hand signals during the period to let you know how well they were progressing. For closure, they showed you how well they had mastered the objective through the use of white boards. Assessment for learning was clear from beginning to end.

Great job!
Barry

Because our classrooms have interior windows, I can see into every classroom, every day, without disrupting the class. Therefore, my visits are not wasted, for example, by observing students while they are taking a test. I will usually plan to be out of my office a class period or two with no set agenda except to see classrooms I haven't visited. In some cases, I stay most of the class period just to witness a new procedure that I can share with other teachers.

Real-Time Coaching

The observational technique I enjoy the most, but use the least, is real-time coaching. An observer has to be very careful using this technique, because if not performed properly, it can be intrusive and make the teacher uncomfortable. Basically, real-time coaching allows the observer the freedom to make or suggest changes during the class. In some cases, I've asked the teacher if I can ask the students some questions or have them perform an activity. At other times, I've passed a note to the teacher during downtime to make a suggestion. The benefit of doing this is that we find out immediately if something works rather than wondering about it in the post-observation conference.

Example of Real-Time Coaching

Sheree Lester is an excellent teacher who uses many of the techniques that I mentioned in Chapters 3 and 4. While observing her class one day, I noticed that she used a variety of ways to check for student learning during the period. The objective was to have students compare and contrast the three main Western religions by filling in a table. As the lesson progressed, I became curious to know how much the students knew prior to entering the class. I gave Sheree a note while the students were doing independent work at their seats. The note read, "If you get a chance at the end of the period, please ask the students how many cells they could have filled in at the beginning of class." She did this, and the result was twofold. First, the students demonstrated a wide range of prior knowledge—some had little understanding, whereas one could have filled in the entire table before class started. This led to a discussion of differentiated instruction during our post-observation conversation. Second, Sheree could see how much learning occurred during the period by comparing students' preperformances with their postperformances. Sheree was pleasantly surprised. A side effect was that students were able to see how much they learned.

A negative aspect of real-time coaching is that the teacher could become defensive or be thrown off her anticipated course of action. In order for this coaching to work, the teacher must know that I value her ability but sometimes need to seize the moment to determine if an alternative might produce positive results. To avoid negative side effects, I often ask teachers to carry out my suggestion in the next class period (assuming the conditions are the same). This gives the teacher time to think about the suggestion rather than have to make changes on the run. The teacher may even suggest a course of action that's better than my original suggestion. The results of the experiment often lead our discussion during the next phase of the process, the *learning conversation*, which I describe in Chapter 6.

What's the Point?

- Many studies show a positive correlation between student engagement and achievement.
- Traditional observation procedures focus on teacher behaviors.
- Learner observation focuses on the behaviors of students.

6

Learning Conversations

Essential Question: What is the best way for an observer to provide feedback to a teacher following a classroom observation?

The collection of information conveyed during a lesson is useless unless it can stimulate teacher growth or help administrators make future employment decisions. It's unfortunate that many administrators neglect the importance of this post-observation activity and assume that a one-size-fits-all conferencing technique is satisfactory. The first thing an administrator needs to consider is whether the objective of the observation and conference is to promote professional growth or to gather documentation that will support a decision to terminate the teacher. Professional development—clearly the more beneficial purpose of evaluation—regrettably has less formal support in schools.

For the purpose of this chapter, I limit my discussion to the use of observation and conferencing to stimulate professional growth. In Chapter 8, I discuss the process of eliminating unsatisfactory performance.

Traditional Approaches

Some teachers don't even have conferences—they simply get a review in their boxes at the end of the year. Many post-observation conferences that do occur follow a similar pattern. During the conference, the administrator may ask a few questions, but she usually dominates the conversation, going over what she liked and what she thinks the teacher should change in the future. A hierarchy is established that causes the teacher to sit and listen rather than try to enter into the discussion.

As a novice administrator, I often held post-observation conferences that were not productive. This occurred for the following reasons:

- I often dominated the airtime and tried to correct everything in one conference. I wanted to "teach" the teachers rather than help them learn. I tried to drag teachers down my path rather than guide them down theirs. As with ineffective teaching, I had a certain amount of information that I wanted to cover regardless of how much learning occurred.
- The success of the conference was determined by "feeling" tones (amicable versus argumentative, for instance) rather than by evidence of learning. I discovered that it was much easier to focus on what went well than to suggest improvements. Especially with stubborn teachers, I would sometimes back off what I really wanted to say so as to avoid confrontation. If the teacher left the conference in a decent mood, I felt the experience was a success.
- In some cases, I had not planned properly for the conference. Like teaching, holding a successful conference takes planning. Commendations and recommendations must be backed up with specific observed behaviors. The observer must be ready to provide concrete examples regarding how certain recommendations could be met. When a teacher asks, "How

do I do that?" the observer had better be able to provide a worthwhile response.

Conversing with the Brain in Mind

As leaders seek meaningful models of professional development, the new field of cognitive neuroscience is gaining attention. Summative and formative evaluations that rely on the carrot-and-stick method of supervision are giving way to learning conversations for professional growth, and cognitive theories of learning and memory can inform these conversations. Learning to meld cognitive theories with the best instructional practices and professional growth presents a major challenge for instruction leaders. (Hurley, Greenblatt, & Cooper, 2003, p. 31)

In Chapter 1, I presented information connecting brain research to learning. This information is valuable to teachers and administrators as we examine the process of teaching. It must also be considered by administrators as they work with teachers to help them continue to improve. This goal—continuous improvement—must be kept in mind at all times. Teachers who feel that the observer comes into their classrooms to find something wrong won't benefit from the process. I have never had a teacher inform me that improvement wasn't possible, that they had already reached perfection.

A constructivist view that's beneficial for student learning can also be effective in conversations with teachers. If the administrator merely wants to have the teacher repeat the recommendations that he provides, then checking for prior knowledge isn't necessary. However, it has been pointed out that this will limit retention and make any change in behavior unlikely. If the purpose is to sustain long-term improvement, administrators must start by considering the knowledge, skills, and attitudes that the teacher brings to the conversation. As Searfoss and Enz note (citing Walen and DeRose, 1993), "The traditional checklist with nary a mention of integrated teaching approaches has become a conspicuous dinosaur in American schools" (1996, p. 38).

I have often said that I would rather guide a teacher down her path than drag her down mine. Some teachers need much reinforcement before they will consider suggestions for improvement. Others need very little reinforcement and want to jump right in with how they could have done a better job. A teacher who's struggling with classroom discipline doesn't want to hear how she could have used more individualized instruction. She's looking for help with survival, not with refinement.

The level of concern that the teacher feels will have an effect on her learning. If the teacher feels threatened or uncomfortable, she could spend the conference time either arguing or sitting passively and waiting for the negative experience to end. As Caine and Caine note, "Where there is stress, there is neurological 'downshifting' to basic survival mode, sacrificing higher-order thinking" (1994, p. 34). On the other hand, teachers who don't care about the result of the conference may tune out the administrator, feeling that they have little to gain. Or maybe they do care but don't feel that the administrator has anything to offer. The teacher who attends the conference with no paper and pen often sends a message that she thinks there probably won't be anything worthwhile to record or there will be so little that she can remember it. I take pleasure when a teacher reflects and then asks for paper and pen so that the thought doesn't escape her. This might be a clever device to stroke my ego, but it works. One of the most satisfying results of a learning conversation for both participants occurs when the teacher is challenged to improve and she develops strategies to accomplish that task.

Like their students, teachers have various learning styles. Some teachers are able to analyze the lesson very nicely as a result of their own reflection and the conversation with the administrator. Others will benefit from seeing the lesson presented in an outline, timeline, graph, or other organizer. Frequency charts are very meaningful to many teachers because teachers often don't see the cumulative effect of their actions. To tell a teacher that she took up a lot of airtime is not as effective as showing her a chart that records the amount of teacher talk versus student talk. Quite often, it's sufficient to let the teacher see the chart and make her own conclusions.

Another aspect of teacher learning to consider is the amount of information that teachers can take away from the conversation. Administrators who have a "coverage" mentality will be as ineffective as the teachers who use this philosophy in the classroom. This is especially true for new teachers, who typically have multiple areas needing attention. They should be presented with information in small chunks followed by time to reflect. Teachers shouldn't be overloaded with everything the administrator can think of to address. The focus should be on two or three areas of strength and two or three areas in which improvement can be achieved.

In order for learning to occur, the teacher needs to be engaged in the conversation. If the administrator dominates airtime, the benefits for the teacher are reduced. One of the great ironies that I witness occurs when the observer lectures to the teacher about how she needs to engage her students. Probing questions can cause the teacher to reflect much more than can the administrator's preaching.

The importance of meaning in learning was discussed in Chapter 1. If the teacher doesn't see how the recommendations affect her subject or grade, she will be unlikely to put them into long-term memory. She must see how the recommendations will make her a better teacher and help her students learn; a band teacher might completely ignore examples culled from English classes, for instance, and might argue that English teachers don't have only one planning period to prepare for teaching both novices and experts who are playing 10 different instruments.

Providing expectations for instruction prior to the observation can be very effective. The administrator should make his expectations known in a variety of ways. First, guidelines for instruction and assessment should be listed in the faculty handbook. (It has always amazed me to see very specific guidelines for teachers regarding discipline and other operational items but very little regarding planning, teaching, and assessing.) Second, the principal, assistant principals, and teachers who present at faculty meetings at the beginning of the year should model effective instructional techniques. Lecturing teachers as to how they should engage their students isn't effective.

Pre-Observation Conversations

Pre-observation conversations should be an option for all teachers. Meeting with teachers new to the building at the beginning of the year to discuss instruction can be very beneficial. In particular, administrators shouldn't assume that veteran teachers who are new to their building already possess the skills and knowledge expected from all teachers. Again, this should be a discussion, not a lecture. This meeting can relieve some of the fears that teachers might have about the first observation. Discussing what the teacher might do during the lesson in a pre-observation conversation can be more effective than telling the teacher later what she should have done. Pre-observation conversations create partnerships between teachers and administrators; post-observation conferences without prior communication often alienate the teacher and the administrator.

Below are some questions that the administrator could ask in a pre-observation conversation:

- "What is it that you want the students to be able to do by the end of the lesson?"
- "How will you engage the students during the class period in the accomplishment of the objective?"
- "How will you know before, during, and after the lesson which students have mastered the objective?"
- "How will you differentiate instruction based on your assessment for learning?"
- "Are you trying anything new?"
- "What obstacles do you expect?"
- "What would you like me to look for during the lesson?"

Post-Observation Conferences

The setting for the post-observation conference is important. I never sit at my desk when conferencing with a teacher: The principal's desk signals a position of power that's important in some situations but can be detrimental to collegial discussions. Instead, I ask the teacher to join me at comfortable seating in another area of the office where there's no barrier between us. I face the teacher and try to signal openness with my body posture. Sometimes, I find it effective to meet in the teacher's classroom. This puts the discussion on her turf and can make her feel more comfortable. Another advantage is that we can discuss the way the classroom was arranged and re-create events in a more realistic manner. The disadvantage is that I lose access to supplementary information that I might want to share, such as previous observations or instructional resources, unless I bring that with me.

An effective post-observation conference should simulate effective instruction. The administrator should plan for it. However, care has to be taken to make sure that too much time does not expire between the observation and the conference. I would suggest that no more than two days separate the two events. In planning, the administrator should determine the objectives that he hopes to meet by the end of the conference. I typically try to have the teacher list two to three areas of strength and two to three areas in which she wants to continue to improve. Also, the plan should include how the teacher will be engaged in the discussion and how the administrator will assess whether or not the objective has been met. Sound familiar?

The conference technique that I use is structured but has room for variation depending on the information provided by the teacher. The conference basically has four parts:

- Teacher reaction
- My clarifying questions
- My observations and recommendations

- Closure by the teacher listing commendations and recommendations

Before I get into the structured part of the conference, I check the emotional state of the teacher. This can be accomplished by asking, "How is life treating you?" If the teacher is, for example, worried about an ailing parent, I need to show concern for her emotional state before we analyze the lesson. Some teachers have been relieved when we postpone the conversation until after they deal with more important issues.

Teacher Reaction

As with classroom instruction, it's important to check for prior knowledge. I follow the icebreaker by asking the teacher to tell me how the lesson went. "What went well?" "Now that you have had time to reflect, what would you do differently next time?" I have found it unproductive to ask them *if* they would change anything. They often say no. Asking them *what* they will change lets them know that reflection and continuous improvement are expected, not just hoped for.

In addition, I always have the teacher open and close the conference. The only exception is if I haven't provided the process that I use for the conference. If that's the case, I'll explain the process and then turn it over to the teacher.

Clarifying Questions

Following the first segment of teacher talk, which is focused on the teacher's feelings, I ask clarifying questions to help us both analyze the lesson. Many years ago, I would routinely have to ask, "What was the objective of the lesson?" Now this is the exception, rather than the rule, because the teacher has already made the objective evident during the class. Some examples of questions I might ask include the following:

- "How well did the students react to the brainstorming activity you used?"
- "How did you decide which students to assign to each group?"
- "How did you extend the learning that occurred today through their homework assignment?"
- "In regard to wandering, watching, working, and learning, how would you describe the behaviors of the students during the class period? What evidence did you find that they were learning?"

The key to making this work is that the questions should be designed to gather more information if needed and to get the teacher to reflect, rather than to put her on the defensive. An example of a question destined to lead to confrontation is, "Did you notice how many students were off task?" Questioning of this type puts the teacher on the defensive and should be avoided.

My Observations and Recommendations

The next segment is my talk time. I explain to the teacher that I see my role as being another set of eyes. I don't pretend to be the holder of all knowledge and wisdom who has come to make her a great teacher. My goal is to initiate a discussion that will lead to continued improvement. I share with her what I think I saw during the observation. My tally of the student behaviors is an approximation, as I cannot positively identify the actions of all students at all times. The Learner Observation Summary in Chapter 5 serves as the focal point of our discussion. The teacher should already be familiar with the form, but I review what it shows from my perspective. I refer to my script to highlight specific events in an effort to add detail to the events listed on the form. In some cases, I fill out the form after the conversation because I want the teacher to help me identify which student behaviors occurred during the lesson. Once again, what's important is the conversation that is held, not the documentation that accompanies it.

I initiate the conversation by discussing the evidence of learning (or lack of such) that I witnessed, not the strategies used by the teacher. When learning was evident, I point out the strategies the teacher used to cause this to happen. When it was apparent that students didn't master the objective, we discuss the strategies that were used and ways that more progress could have been made. Often, there's a disconnect between the objective, the activities, and the assessment. In the past, teachers and I would spend a great deal of time discussing what students really needed to know or to be able to do by the end of the class period. When the state and local curriculum guides provide specific objectives, this is less of a problem. Having all teachers plan together has also made this less of an area for concern. Teachers catch each other during common planning saying, "That is really an activity, not an objective." Currently, the discussion focuses more on ways to get all students to master the objective than on the objective itself.

During this segment of the post-observation conversation, I point out the teacher behavior that led to students' mastering of the objective. I stay away from soft feedback, such as "I liked how you called on every student" or "It was a good lesson that students enjoyed." Specific feedback gives the teacher more to take from the conference. For example, "When you provided wait time, the number of correct responses doubled" or "During the cooperative learning exercise, half of the students were wandering." When making recommendations, I typically cite examples of what I have seen to be effective in other classrooms that the teacher might want to try. I am careful when using the name of any one teacher because this often can breed animosity. Upon request, I will recommend other teachers who are trying similar things and leave it up to the teacher to decide who she will observe. A statement that should be avoided at all costs is, "When I taught I used to . . . ."

Closure by the Teacher

During the last segment, the teacher talks. I ask *her* to provide the commendations and recommendations. Sometimes she repeats what she said in the beginning of the conference, but this is uncommon. Typically, she'll reach a different conclusion from that reached earlier, either through her own reflection of the lesson or after considering the information that I presented. This is how I check to see if she mastered the objective I had for the conference. The goal, however, is not that she come up with the same commendations and recommendations as I do. The goal is that she be able to determine some of the things that caused student learning and that she identify areas in which she can improve student learning. If I feel that she has missed something, I will wait until the next observation to verify my assumptions.

Specific timelines should be agreed upon for the application of recommendations: "Some time in the next two weeks, I would like you to invite me back to see you try that out." Without a timeline, the teacher will often fall back into her routine and forget what was discussed in the conference.

Using the post-observation technique described above, many teachers now look at the results and ask me how they can get more students learning. Teachers now start the conference with "I didn't see as much learning as I would have liked" or "I need to find a way to challenge the students who get it right away while I work with those who struggle." A teacher who tells me that five students mastered the objective at the beginning of the lesson and 10 didn't "have it" by the end is ready for a discussion of differentiated instruction. Teachers now know the process and analyze the lesson long before they reach my door. My role is to provide data and then let them react. In the best-case scenario, the teacher decides what she needs to do to improve, and my job is merely to support her efforts with some suggestions.

Keeping Track

It's been my experience that most post-observation conferences occur in isolation. By that I mean that the conversation includes only the most recent lesson. In the spring, many administrators don't look at the conclusion that was reached in the fall; reaching back to conferences in previous years is unheard of. Formal evaluations are sent to the central office, where they sit in a file that no one ever reviews. Administrators come and go. Even if the same team stays in a building for a few years, they switch the teachers they observe. This means that it wouldn't be unlikely for a teacher with 20 years of experience to have feedback from 10 to 15 administrators. It's possible that the same recommendation could be made following 40 conferences (assuming two per year). It's also possible that 40 different recommendations could be made. If the teacher changes schools, the disconnect between observations becomes even more likely—and this is assuming that the teacher gets feedback twice a year. Many teachers report going years with no observations. This situation encourages a "this too shall pass" mentality. Veteran teachers soon learn to sit there and nod in agreement because something new will be discussed in the next conference. (I wonder how many of us would continue seeing a doctor who made no effort to examine our medical history.) The "Teacher Recommendation Summary" in Figure 6.1 shows a quick and easy way to document recommendations made over a period of time.

To have a history of recommendations made to teachers is useless unless something occurs based on the results. This list of recommendations should provide direction for individual and school goals (which I discuss in Chapter 8). Professional development should be designed to strengthen the areas noted as needing improvement. For example, assume that the majority of the teachers had "increase ways you see mastery of the objective" as one of their recommendations.

FIGURE 6.1
Sample Teacher Recommendation Summary

	Planning		Instruction		Assessment		Management
P1	Have daily plans (dated for the day) stating specific objective to be mastered that day.	I1	Make the objective known to the students throughout the class period.	A1	Check prior knowledge.	M1	Develop routines that reduce the need for teacher directives.
P2	Plan a variety of questioning techniques.	I2	Engage students in order to reduce watching.	A2	Increase ways that the class can demonstrate mastery of the objective.	M2	Eliminate talking when someone else has the floor.
P3	Plan activities for students who complete work early.	I3	Use techniques to motivate students.	A3	Provide for student closure.	M3	Organize tasks for smooth transitions.
P4	Plan for daily assessment, group checking for understanding, pre-during-post.	I4	Vary instructional techniques to accommodate different learning styles.	A4	Use assessment for learning techniques during the class period.	M4	Respond to misbehavior appropriately.
P5	Make sure objective is at an appropriate level of difficulty.	I5	Vary instructional techniques to accommodate different achievement levels.	A5	Involve the students through self-assessment.	M5	Create urgency for student by monitoring the quality of process or product.
P6	Specify instructional procedures in plans (not Review for Test) for mastery of the objective(s).	I6	Provide guidelines for group activities.	A6	Minimize calling on the first hand up and moving on.		

FIGURE 6.1 *(cont.)*
Sample Teacher Recommendation Summary

	Planning		Instruction		Assessment		Management
P7	Identify specific SOLs to be mastered.	**I7**	Watch the process that groups use before moving to help them with content.	**A7**	Assess using a variety of levels of Bloom's taxonomy.		
P8	Plan for closure.	**I8**	Establish routines to minimize downtime.	**A8**	Analyze the tasks, and check progress at each step.		
P9	Include long-range planning.	**I9**	Reduce time spent copying notes.				
P10	Plan five days in advance.						
P11	Plan for differentiated instruction.						

Teacher	Fall 03	Spring 04	Fall 04	Spring 05
Teacher A			A2	A4, A2
Teacher B	A4	I2, M3	I5	I4
Teacher C			P1, P6, A4	A4
Teacher D	I4	I5	P4	I2

A valuable professional development activity would have teachers work together to address this recommendation. The only time a history of recommendations is kept is when the teacher is deemed to be incompetent. On some occasions, administrators will meet at the beginning of the year to share their opinions regarding who is unsatisfactory. The performance history for all teachers needs to be regularly discussed, not just the history of the unsatisfactory teachers.

Keeping a history of recommendations isn't valuable unless there's consistency among observers regarding the process. Principal preparation programs typically address observing but not conferencing. I was able to find very little in my research of books and periodicals regarding post-observation conferences. I know of no principal (including myself) who has been observed holding a post-observation conference with a teacher as part of *his* evaluation. I also know of no principal (except myself) who observes his assistant principals in conference with teachers. For many administrators, the only training that relates to holding a post-observation conference is the experience they received while going through the process as a teacher.

I am amazed that very few administrators ever receive feedback on one of the most important aspects of their jobs. I have observed and held conversations with my assistant principals and department heads (high school only) every year that I have been a principal. Many of the conferences that I have observed, involving my own staff or principals from other schools, are conversations that often wander with no clear objective. The administrator usually dominates airtime, and the goal is process-oriented, with no identification of a desired product.

Peer observations are not just a good idea for teachers. In working with other administrators, I have seen remarkable improvement after pointing out to them that learning conversations should contain the qualities of effective instruction. In addition, I have learned much about holding productive conferences with teachers by watching other administrators and having them watch me and provide feedback. I have also found it extremely beneficial to meet with the other administrators in my building following observations to share our findings with each other. This increases inter-rater reliability and helps us develop a common vocabulary and understanding of what effective teaching and learning look like. Although I don't do it nearly enough, one of the most valuable activities I have experienced occurred when another administrator and I observed the same lesson and then discussed how we might hold the learning conversation.

What's the Point?

- Traditional post-observation conferences ignore brain-based learning principles and are designed for hire/fire decisions rather than for professional growth.
- Learning conversations are centered on principles of how people learn about and reflect on effective teaching methods.

7

Teacher Learning

Essential Question: What is the best way to provide professional growth opportunities for teachers that increase their abilities to help students learn and that keep them in the profession?

Teacher Shortage

Over 13 percent of teachers leave education each year, compared to 11 percent of professionals in other occupations. Of new teachers, 29 percent leave in the first three years and 39 percent in the first five years (Viadero in Heller, 2004). Halford (1998) suggests that we are a profession that eats its young. Further, we have fewer people who want to enter the teaching profession. Of those who do, we aren't able to hire some because of increased requirements, and most of those we do hire leave within the first three to five years. This sounds like a crisis to me.

Some of the causes of this are beyond the control of anyone at the building level. However, much can be done at this level to address another problem: retaining the good teachers we have. We may need to spend less time on recruitment and more time on training our current teachers. A lack of professional development isn't often cited as a reason teachers leave the profession, but training can help teachers address the reasons that do cause them to leave. Among other reasons, many teachers leave the profession because they feel isolated; having them work together in groups, along with using peer observations and study groups, can minimize this problem. Teachers new to a building have told me that nonteaching requirements are the most stressful. Learning new procedures for grading, dealing with discipline, special education, attendance, and planning place additional pressures on teachers.

Teacher Training

In most schools, professional development for new and veteran teachers has similar characteristics. New teachers go through an orientation provided by the school district before school starts; most topics center on special education, license information, and benefits such as health care and insurance. Although this information is very important for all employees to know, new teachers often complain that they want to spend this valuable time preparing for the first days of school.

After a few days of professional development by the district, new teachers are sent to their prospective schools to obtain more specialized training. Typically, all teachers new to the building receive the same dose of training regardless of their levels of experience. The first day they report to work, all teachers meet in the library, auditorium, or cafeteria to be introduced to new staff. All teachers then receive instruction about the policies and procedures of the district and the individual school as administrators read the staff handbook. Other meetings, designed to acquaint teachers with the hot topic for the year—cooperative learning, differentiated instruction, problem-based learning, high-yield strategies, and so on—consume the remainder of the day. This exposure is provided by administrators, outside experts, or, in some cases, other teachers selected because of their willingness or abilities to address the subject at hand.

The content of these sessions often focuses on the theory rather than on the delivery. Teachers leave with little understanding of how to apply what they have learned. Every three years or so, many teachers are exposed to team-building exercises designed to get them to know each other and learn to work together to accomplish school goals. For many, this is the only time all year they communicate with other teachers, unless they are in the same department or lunch group. During these sessions, many teachers think about all the things they could be doing in their classrooms to get ready for the first day of school.

During the year, most schools have one or more days or half days of professional development. The topic may be similar to the one presented at the beginning of the year, or it may be something completely different. Rarely do teachers have input in the planning or implementation of these sessions. Faculty meetings usually don't address professional development topics. They are designed for the transmittal of "administrivia," which can often be handled best through e-mail.

New teachers get the following message: "Here is your class-room, your textbook, your roster of students, and the bell schedule. You have three years to get it right." They typically have to develop their own plans and tests even though a seasoned veteran has it all next door. Plans and tests that have been tweaked year after year are just out of reach of the new teacher. Strategies for time management, dealing with disruptive students, and communicating with parents are equally unobtainable. What makes matters worse is the practice of assigning the most challenging students to the newest teachers, who have the least chance of success. Veteran teachers feel they have earned the right to teach the advanced students. Each new teacher has to reinvent the wheel on her own. If she wants to lament all of the problems associated with her profession, a lounge is waiting nearby where discourse of this nature is common. However, solutions are not shared because this is part of the process of survival of the fittest. It's unfortunate that increasing numbers of new teachers quit rather than fight the battle alone. Remember, we eat our young.

Reality Sets In

After all the initial meetings and review of the propaganda describing how things should be within the school, the new teacher gets a dose of reality. She sees how the other teachers dress, the time they arrive and depart from school, and how much work they carry home with them each evening. She also notes how they deal with students in the hall or listens as she passes by their classrooms. The chatter in the teachers' lounge colors her initial impression of the school following her induction. The procedures listed in the handbook give way to the examples she sees every day. It's the behavior of the inhabitants of the school that dictates its culture. This is especially true regarding professional growth.

In some schools, a review of the culture indicates that teachers survive professional development but do little to change traditional practices. In many cases, the principal models this behavior by suffering through his own professional development and troubling teachers with their professional development only because it's required by the central office. Principals who avoid professional growth opportunities for themselves send a clear message to their staffs that the status quo is acceptable. In school cultures such as these, professional development is something that's done to you rather than something you do for yourself.

The Project on the Next Generation of Teachers at the Harvard Graduate School of Education suggests that new teachers need much more than they are currently getting in most schools: "What new teachers want in their induction is experienced colleagues who will take their daily dilemmas seriously, watch them teach and provide feedback, help them develop instructional strategies, model skilled teaching and share insights about students' work and lives. What new teachers need is sustained, school-based professional development" (Johnson & Kardos, 2002, p. 12).

New Teachers

Obviously, new teachers have different needs than do veteran teachers. What many don't realize, however, is that there's often a wide range of needs within the group of new teachers. Some may have taught for years but are new to the building, district, or state. Some may have had extensive training in theory and practice in their preparation programs. Some may have taken the fast track available for career switchers that often can be accomplished during the summer. Forty-six percent of new teachers in New Jersey were career changers who were, on average, 35 years old (Johnson & Kardos, 2002). These teachers will have different needs than will those just out of college who might be mistaken for students.

At the end of each interview of a prospective hire, I ask the candidate what questions he has of me. The most frequently asked question is, "What programs do you have to help new teachers?" Veteran teachers who are new to the building also ask this because they realize that being successful in a new school requires more than knowledge of instructional techniques. Prior to this point, I express my expectations to the candidate. In an effort to lower their level of concern, I explain all of the resources that are available to them to help them meet those expectations. I divide my response into two parts: the programs we have for new teachers, and the programs we have for all teachers.

Professional Development Programs for New Teachers

We can offer new teachers much more if they're hired in the spring rather than when school isn't in session. In rare cases, we have been able to bring new teachers in as substitutes prior to their full-time employment. Ideally, I would like this to occur for all new teachers. In some cases, either I or the teacher see that the fit is not a positive one. It's better to find this out in the spring than wait until after the first quarter of the school year has passed. If all goes well, the teacher can begin his first year with some of the hurdles out of the way. If substitute teaching is not an option, the teacher can at least meet some of the current teachers and get a feel for how business is conducted with students in attendance. If the applicant is hired during the summer, we do our best to pair him with a teacher in the same department and grade. Having that resource prior to the first reporting date takes a great deal of stress off new teachers.

After the district meetings during the first two reporting dates, all new teachers to my school meet with LuAnne Dow. LuAnne is a mathematics teacher who has been our lead mentor for two years. She is trained for her role and has a cadre of teachers trained to mentor new teachers. At the first meeting, she explains the various components of the mentor program. The goal of the program is to provide support for new teachers and to introduce them to the culture of the school. Some topics address big questions, such as "What do I need to do in order to be an effective teacher at this school?" Other topics address more immediate questions, such as "How do I get the password to check my e-mail?" The agenda is a mixture of predetermined topics and questions from the audience. Teachers sit in a circle, as this encourages participation and breaks down any feeling of hierarchy. Snacks and decorations communicate a friendly environment. No questions are dumb questions.

At the first meeting, the assistant principals share some nuts and bolts regarding the operation of the school. Prior to this, new teachers have read the handbook, so the administrators merely help with interpretation rather than go over it page by page. The main goal is for teachers to see the administrators as a resource to help them succeed. Other key people are brought in for introduction, such as the media specialist and the technology coordinator. As with the meeting with the assistant principals, the goal is to provide a resource and to initiate a discussion rather than to honor the new teachers with sessions from "distinguished lecturers."

Somewhere during the initial meetings, I join the group to discuss instructional expectations and the process of learner observations and evaluation. A few years ago, I would hold a pre-observation conversation with each teacher for this purpose. Meeting with all of them at once has been more efficient and has allowed us the time to discuss specific lessons in pre-observation conversations. In this meeting, I explain my role as another set of eyes, what I look for during an observation or walk-through, how I hold the post-observation conference, and any paperwork that is involved along the way. In some respects, I think the teachers gain comfort knowing that they are all in the same boat and can share their experiences, both positive and negative, with other professionals. I always leave time to answer any questions or concerns they have.

The most productive aspect of my visit probably occurs after I leave. It's fortunate that my ego can stand the hit, because soon after my visit, LuAnne spends time with the new teachers reassuring them that I visit classrooms to help them grow and not just to look for what went wrong. She tells them that the lesson could bomb and I will merely use it as part of a discussion for continuous improvement. She offers her services prior to an observation to ease their fears and provide support. She also offers to review their plans and grade books to make sure they are acceptable.

Subsequent meetings address a variety of topics, such as planning, grading, back-to-school night, peer observations, discipline, and special education. Throughout the process, new teachers are encouraged to give feedback regarding the events of the day and the mentoring program. In some cases, teachers ask for different topics to be covered. Sometimes, they get stressed over deadlines, so new teacher meetings are postponed. LuAnne provides a balance between "Here is what *I think* you need" and "What do *you think* you need?"

I recently asked the new teachers to evaluate their experiences as new teachers at our school. They unanimously praised the mentor program and had some good suggestions. Some said they needed the information regarding special education earlier. Others said that we needed to provide more specific information regarding procedures, such as timeout and social probation. The key to having a successful mentoring program is to get to new teachers early and often and then back off as appropriate.

Some of the praise addressed professional development programs that we have for all teachers. I describe those in the remainder of this chapter.

Professional Development Programs for All Teachers

Collaboration

The key components of our teacher learning program recognize the benefits of sharing. Our mentor teachers share their expertise with new teachers rather than the new teachers having to wait years to figure it all out on their own. In fact, one new teacher said she was shocked when a veteran teacher gave her a month of plans to get her started at the beginning of the year. She was thus able to focus on how to teach and how to complete the other requirements of the day.

This isn't true only with new teachers. All but a few of the teachers at my school plan together on a regular basis. Most assessments are common when the subject and grade level are the same. The benefits of this sharing are enormous, as three minds contribute to the process rather than each teacher existing in isolation.

As a novice administrator, I exposed my teachers to professional development regarding the construction of tests. I have recently found it to be more productive to have teachers of common grade levels and subjects construct and evaluate their own tests. When their students don't do well, these teachers often realize that the questions were poorly worded or the test didn't assess the intended outcomes. Teachers now go back to daily objectives and informal assessments to determine why students performed the way they did. They then share results and discuss strategies they used to help students be successful. These events are rare when teachers work in isolation.

Peer Observations

The benefits of sharing are amplified by peer observations. In Chapter 5, I discussed the learner observations that are performed by administrators. Six years ago, I suggested the idea of peer observations to my department heads. My suggestion was met with much resistance: "Some teachers don't like to be observed," "We don't want to be administrators," "We don't have enough time," "It would only be helpful to see our subject taught." I decided at the time that there were other issues I needed to address rather than force peer observations down the teachers' throats. Two years ago, our school eliminated teaming in two of the three grades. The team-planning period became a duty period. Teachers were told that this could not be another planning period, nor was it to be another teaching period that required planning. Some schools used this time to man the hallways, bathrooms, and cafeteria with supervisors, among other duties.

My thought was that this was a good time to provide professional development, student assistance, and peer observations in addition to some limited supervisory duties. I required all teachers with duty periods (approximately one-third of the faculty) to observe a fellow teacher during the first nine-week marking period. The only requirement was that they leave a nice note for the teacher and let me know when the observation had been completed. (I also asked them to see what learning was evident during their visits, but I didn't expect them to share this with the teachers they observed.) Many of the teachers sent their colleagues a positive e-mail that they copied to me.

The results were amazing. My only regret was that I waited so long to get it going. I asked each teacher if the experience was worthwhile. The response was 100 percent positive. Some teachers expressed their desire to continue the process the next quarter. I decided to expand it to the other teachers in the school, and the guidance counselors decided on their own to join in. Now, when a parent or student talks about a class, the counselor can often say, "I've been there." Even though some of the elective teachers have only one planning period, I have heard no complaints. In fact, I offered to bring in substitutes for those who needed them, but no one has taken me up on my offer. I allow the teachers a week to decide whom they want to see, and then I assign the rest. Many assignments are totally random: The geometry teacher might observe the art teacher; the French teacher might see the physical education teacher.

Some teachers see what their students do in other classes. Some teachers see what other teachers in their subject areas do before the students come to them. The greatest indicator of success that I have seen is a teacher using a new technique to get students learning. "I saw you using flash cards to check understanding. When did you start doing that?" "Right after I visited Nancy's class and saw her using them so effectively." Some day, the Teacher of the Year may be selected because those who vote for her have seen her teach. Wouldn't that be something?

The teachers experienced an enhanced pride in the school as they marveled over the expertise and dedication of their colleagues. They were also experiencing professional growth in a meaningful and satisfying way. I now require all teachers to observe other teachers at least two to four times a year depending on their number of nonteaching periods. The quality of the teachers ensures that any observation will be positive. I would have to adjust this procedure if some of my teachers weren't doing a good job.

Common Planning

In addition to peer observations, teachers can use their duty periods for common planning. This has helped many teachers because individual planning still needs to occur to a certain extent. It would be hard to fit it all into one duty period. Many teachers use this period for professional research. All I ask is that they document the topics of research in their logs. In some cases, I provide the source; in others, the teacher selects. For example, I asked all the teachers to read Carol Tomlinson's *The Differentiated Classroom: Responding to the Needs of All Learners* (1999) prior to having them meet in groups to discuss it. Many teachers use the time to catch up on current teaching strategies or to learn more specific techniques for their subject areas.

When we do have time for whole-group professional development, it's typically planned and conducted by teachers in our school. However, this never happens on the first day teachers report: That day, we have a welcoming breakfast and then teachers are on their own to socialize, find out what others did during the summer, and begin to get their classrooms ready. With almost all professional development opportunities, teachers are given the opportunity to provide topics of interest to them. The list of these topics is presented to teachers so that they can choose their first, second, and third preferences. Based on these results, some topics make it and some don't. Finding presenters and facilitators is done after the teachers make their selections, as opposed to the common practice of finding a good presenter and being limited to his subject. Feedback is always obtained to guide future professional development.

Modeling

I see my role as that of both the leader of learning and the lead learner. If I ask the teachers to read and discuss an article or book, I must do the same. At least once a month, I share an article or Web site with them that I think is valuable. This saves time for them to research good material, and it sends a message that I need to learn as much as they do. I attend the sessions that teachers conduct for others, ask questions, and take notes. I am there as a learner, not as a supervisor. My office is filled with books and professional journals that I frequently share with my faculty. I let them know that I spend as much time as I can in the classroom because that's where I learn about effective teaching.

We should practice what we preach. How many times have teachers sat though lectures on the topic of engaging the audience? How many times have they been exposed to the same activities designed to teach them about differentiated instruction regardless of their levels of readiness or interest? How many times have they been exposed to Gardner's multiple intelligences from "experts" using only one method of delivery? I wonder what would happen if a presenter used group checking for understanding before, during, and after a discussion of assessment for learning. I have also seen principals use PowerPoint presentations describing how to use technology with slides that are so cluttered and small that only the front row of attendees can read them. We cannot expect teachers to change their practices when principals and teacher trainers continue to use the same methods of working with their learners that have been used for decades, ignoring what is known about how people learn.

Figure 7.1 is a learner plan for a faculty meeting that I held at the beginning of the year. The meeting was different from traditional faculty meetings in the following ways:

- There was a plan for teacher learning, not just an agenda that listed activities.
- The teachers were told what they could expect to learn by the end of the session.
- Assessment for learning was accomplished through group checking for understanding before, during, and after the activity. There was a plan for any of the teachers who were able to show mastery at the beginning of the lesson, as well as a plan for teachers who hadn't mastered the objective by the end of the lesson.
- It was differentiated. New teachers had different activities than did the veterans. The assistant principals charted the behaviors of the teachers during the activity because they were already knowledgeable of the content. Even the homework assignment was differentiated, as new teachers and veteran teachers had different tasks.
- The plan provided ways for the teachers to be overtly engaged in the accomplishment of the objective almost the entire meeting. My job was to facilitate, not to present. My airtime was limited compared to that of my audience.
- The teachers, not the facilitator, performed closure.

FIGURE 7.1
Sample Learner Plan for Faculty Meeting

Title: Review of Tabb Middle School, 03–04		**Content:** Data-driven celebration and planning for improvement	
Grade Level: Teachers	**SOLs:** All	**Date:** August 30	**Time:** 8:00–8:45 a.m.
Objectives: The teacher will be able to: • List three areas of "glow" based on a review of the 03–04 data. • List three areas of "grow" based on a review of the 03–04 data and the goals presented by the SBO and superintendent.		**Resources:** PowerPoint, flash cards, advance organizer.	

Teacher Engagement:
• Have new teachers pass out flash cards and organizers and sit two to each table.
• Start PowerPoint; have teachers write objectives on paper.
• Think/pair/share answers to questions 1–6 and practice (then rapid fire).
• Move to new table.
• Think/pair/share answers to questions 7–9 and practice (then rapid fire).
• Check using flash cards.
• Tell partner three glow/grow w/notes.
• Pass lesson plan out as teachers leave.

Assessment for Learning:
• Raise hands to see if anyone has already mastered obj. (check for prior knowledge).
• Walk about during think/pair/share.
• Flash cards w/out notes.
• Rapid fire.
• Raise your hand if your partner mastered the glow obj., the grow obj.

Differentiation: Check prior knowledge, purposeful seating, movement, new Ts do handouts, APs chart behaviors, alternative homework assignments (AHAs), think/pair/share, advance organizer, individual help from me, practice before rapid fire, choice for most important.

Homework: Retrieve individual data to develop goal.

AHAs:
• APs: Evaluate session.
• New teachers: Use PP on Y drive, and work with mentors.
• Advanced teachers: Evaluate data (unnecessary/missing).

Closure: How were differentiation and assessment for learning evident?

The activity was well received. Some of the veteran teachers picked up on the hidden objective right away, which was to have the "students" (the teachers) discuss the process. I wanted them to be able to see how differentiation and assessment for learning were used during the faculty meeting. This was the first time I used flash cards. I was able to check for understanding along the way even though my "class" contained more than 60 "students." After the faculty meeting, I saw quite a few teachers in the workroom cutting up flash cards. To me, this is evidence of learning. It should happen when teachers work with students, when teachers work with teachers, and when principals work with teachers.

What's the Point?

- Professional development can help teachers address the problems that cause them to leave teaching.
- Observing effective teachers is one of the best ways for teachers to see what works in classrooms.
- Teacher trainers should model effective teaching procedures if they expect instruction to improve.

8

Building a Learning Community

Essential Question: How can the school be organized so that all aspects of it support increased student learning?

Up to this point, the discussion in this book has centered on the classroom. However, many things must go on outside the classroom to cause a culture of learning to exist within the school. The goal should be to establish a learning community that supports what goes on in the classroom. For this goal to be accomplished, the people, procedures, and culture of the learning community must share certain characteristics. Building a learning community takes time. A desire for continuous improvement must be present in every member of the staff. A popular quote is, "If we always do what we have always done, we will always get what we have always gotten." I disagree: In education, if we always do what we have always done, our results will get worse. Parents send us the best students they have, but the students keep changing. Today's students are accustomed to being entertained on demand. To think that we can hold their attention in the same environment that existed even 10 years ago is absurd. This chapter presents some ideas that can institutionalize an emphasis on learning.

The school where I work is not perfect, but I am confident that it would be rated, according to most standards, as at least "good." Our goal is to become great, but we aren't there yet. In an effort to move beyond a discussion of theory, I will provide some examples of what has worked well, what has not worked well, and what we are working on in order to continue to improve.

The People

Collins (2001) studied "good-to-great" organizations from a variety of perspectives. One of his findings was that "good-to-great" leaders "first got the right people on the bus, the wrong people off the bus, and the right people in the right seats—and *then* they figured out where to drive it" (p. 13). I start with a discussion of getting the wrong people off the bus because their seats are often needed in order to get the right people on the bus. Getting the wrong people off the bus is much harder in schools than in many other environments, because we don't have the luxury of giving two weeks' notice to an unsatisfactory employee.

Getting the Wrong People off the Bus

I often hear my colleagues share their frustrations about teachers who are less than satisfactory. They tell me that they would like to do something about it, but they don't have the time or they don't feel their supervisors will support them. It's true that the documentation that's required to dismiss a tenured employee is exhaustive. The process of putting that employee on some type of action plan is also very uncomfortable. Often, the principal must consider the feelings of the rest of the faculty if he comes down hard on "one of their own." It's unfortunate that principals often look the other way to avoid the confrontation and the time it takes to resolve the problem.

My goal has always been for every employee in my building to be good or better. Now, in my 17th year as a principal, this is the first year that I have met that goal. Every year since I became a principal, I had at least one teacher whose performance wasn't satisfactory. One of the measures I use is to ask myself, *Would I want my child in that class?* If the answer is no, I realize that I must do something about the situation. In most cases, it has taken a great deal of time and been very uncomfortable. However, the prolonged effect of an unsatisfactory teacher is worse. Not everyone is meant to teach. Some people lack the necessary personal qualities, and that won't change no matter how much professional development is provided.

As a beginning principal, I was once told to get more documentation to support my requests for action, but I have never had a problem with support from above. I now know not to share those requests until I have collected the proper documentation. I have also never had negative repercussions from my faculty for causing an unsatisfactory teacher to move on. In fact, I have found the opposite to be true. Teachers who are getting the job done don't want someone next door who isn't. Teachers want to be proud not only of what they do but also of the school in general. Principals who talk about how great their school is but allow unsatisfactory teachers to remain that way lose the respect of the other teachers. In addition, removing the person at the bottom of the ladder causes others to improve because a new, higher level of acceptable performance is established.

In Chapter 6, I discussed learning conversations designed to promote professional growth. Conversations also need to occur when teachers aren't meeting expectations. If the principal sees that the performance of a teacher isn't satisfactory, a process needs to be put in place that will cause the person either to change his behavior or to change his location of employment. At the first sign of unacceptable performance, the principal should make his conclusions and expectations for improvement well known. At first, this might mean a conversation and possibly also a follow-up letter that's shared only with the teacher but kept in a file. This letter can be informal, but it should clearly state what prompted it and what needs to change. If this doesn't result in improvement of the teacher's performance, the principal needs to provide more formal documentation that includes very specific directives and time lines. This documentation should be shared with the teacher and reference all previous communications. At this point, a copy should be shared with someone in the human resources department, because if that department doesn't get it in writing, it didn't happen.

At all stages of the process, the principal must be able to document how help was provided. This could include hiring a substitute so that the teacher can observe other teachers. Or, the principal could provide periodicals or books that give specific suggestions that address the identified deficiency. In addition, it's important to involve other professionals early on. The principal should have someone else observe the teacher, such as a specialist from the central office, a department head, or a lead teacher. The purpose of these observations is to provide assistance, not to evaluate the teacher. The principal should be the only person who provides evaluation and directives for improvement—this will reduce confusion for the teacher. Teachers who file grievances when they are recommended for termination typically cite two reasons that they shouldn't lose their jobs: First, they were never told what they were doing wrong. Second, they were given no help in their efforts to improve. This situation can be avoided if the principal follows a specific plan that includes the procedures that I have mentioned. In my experience, principals who say they can't get rid of ineffective teachers haven't used proper procedures. Getting ineffective teachers off the faculty is time consuming and uncomfortable. However, when good teachers replace them, the effort was worthwhile.

Getting the Right People on the Bus

Once the wrong people are off the bus, it's time to get the right people on the bus. As a principal 10 years ago, I knew where to look when I needed a new teacher: I would open a file titled "Applicants," where I would find 10 to 15 applications from prospective teachers. I looked there first because these applicants took the initiative to go beyond the normal procedures to make themselves known to me. I liked this quality. If I didn't find a suitable pool of applicants from this file, I would head to the school board office to search through the voluminous files of prospective teachers contained at that site. I would never need to look beyond the most recent applications to put together a list of highly qualified (by my definition) people to interview. In many cases, the interview process was difficult because I had to choose among so many outstanding individuals. I felt fortunate to be in a school division that had a good reputation and in which teachers wanted to be employed. I had heard about some school divisions that had to hold job fairs to attract applicants and, in some cases, had to travel out of state for recruiting purposes.

Gradually, the circumstances have changed. The good news is that I can now search a database that lists the vital statistics of applicants rather than wade through manila folders. The bad news is that this is necessary because principals must dig much deeper than before to find suitable candidates. I still have a file in my desk drawer, but it contains only a handful of applications. When I go online to search, I sometimes go back two to three years in hopes of finding someone who hasn't been hired. I am hesitant to do this, however, because good teachers get hired on the spot; many school divisions have contracts in hand at job fairs, with signing bonuses and extra pay attached. Last year, I had six teachers retire and five more who moved because of the relocation of their spouses. I spent most of the year searching and interviewing. I am very pleased with the teachers I found, but "the pickin's were slim." It was not until six weeks into the school year that I was fully staffed.

It's well documented that there are fewer candidates in the teacher pool, especially in certain areas. In the past, I would hire provisional or conditional teachers based on their potential, even if they couldn't check off all the boxes regarding their preparation. I focused on the people, not the paperwork. Some of my best teachers didn't have all the education courses or even student teaching experience. This didn't concern me because I could train the right person. However, no amount of training helps a person who doesn't have a love for students and the process of learning.

No Child Left Behind requirements have mandated that all teachers be "highly qualified." This doesn't automatically mean that they are good teachers. It means only that they have taken the correct coursework, completed student teaching, and in many states passed an exam. Some new teachers may have received low marks from cooperating teachers when student teaching, yet they are "highly qualified." The same is true of many experienced teachers who have received years of poor evaluations.

Many college students tell me they want to make money rather than teach. The news of one incident like the tragedy at Columbine High School can be enough to change the minds of many who might otherwise want to enter the teaching profession. In addition, the pressures associated with accountability have increased teacher stress. Now, teachers and administrators are responsible for their products regardless of the factors over which they might have no control. Students come to them with more baggage than in the past, yet teachers are still expected to perform miracles to make the students successful.

The bottom line is that new requirements have made it harder to hire teachers from a pool of applicants that continues to dwindle. Some news reports discuss the looming crisis in education because of the high number of teachers who will soon be retiring. In my opinion, the crisis is already here. When substitutes are increasingly called upon to supervise our classes, we are in a crisis. At the building level, we are limited in our abilities to change hiring policies or increase applicant pools. However, we can do much to keep the good teachers we have and help marginal teachers improve. I'm not suggesting that we continue to employ less-than-satisfactory teachers because of the shortage. In some cases, a good substitute is better than a poor "highly qualified" teacher.

Getting the right people on the bus is one of the most important tasks that a principal faces. The recruiting and interviewing process is critical to the success of the school. The questions asked during the interview should reflect the culture of the school. If a community of learners is desired, the majority of the questions should solicit the applicant's knowledge and feelings about learning. Examples of questions that I have found to be effective include the following:

- **How will you know what to teach?** The applicant's response to this question tells me whether she's aware of national, state, and district standards. One applicant said she couldn't answer the question well because she didn't know what textbook we used. Another applicant said, "Whatever you tell me to teach." I wonder if these people found jobs elsewhere.

- **Pick any topic, and state a daily objective for me.** It's unbelievable how many applicants aren't able to do this. Many of them ramble on about how they taught their favorite lesson, without ever mentioning an objective.

- **At the end of the year, how will you know how well you have done?** The response to this question tells me whether the applicant sets data-driven goals. Some applicants tell me that if they have few failures, they have been successful. If this is their only goal, they could expect less from the students and thereby be even more effective the next year. Some tell me that they want the students to leave with smiles on their faces to signal that they enjoyed being in the class. Of course, low expectations can produce these smiles. Others have told me that students they have taught in the past come back to thank them. This is nice but not exactly statistically significant.

- **What professional reading have you done lately?** The response here tells me whether the teacher is a lifelong learner. Some of my current staff told me in their interviews what they learned by reading works by Marzano, Wong, Wiggins, and Tomlinson. It's unfortunate that a more common response is, "I read a book for the last class I took, but I don't remember the name of it."

- **How will you improve your instructional techniques from year to year?** The applicant's response lets me know whether she has plans for continuous improvement. Teachers I hired gave me the impression that they would be sponges soaking up everything they could from veteran teachers, administrators, courses, conferences, in-house professional development, and professional reading.

- **When you had students fail, why did this happen and what did you do about it?** The response to this question indicates whether the applicant takes ownership of the problem or blames the parents, the students, or the students' previous teachers. It's important to ask the applicant to state what she *did*, not what she would do.

- **How do you assess for learning?** Respondents who tell me about checking for prior knowledge and describe methods for checking for group understanding throughout the lesson get strong consideration. Those who tell me about tests and quizzes at the end of the unit lose ground.

These are just a few of the questions I ask, but they highlight the importance of finding out what the applicant knows and feels about learning. At the end of the interview, I ask the applicant to give me the name of an administrator who has seen her teach. It's discouraging to hear from teachers who are applying from other school divisions that they haven't been observed in two or three years. But I always talk to an administrator when one is available. With rare exception, the mistakes I have made in hiring have occurred when I couldn't compare what I heard in the interview with the opinion of someone who had seen the teacher in action.

Getting the Right People in the Right Seats

Once you have the right people on the bus, you have to get them in the right seats. Teachers have various roles within the organization of the school. Some keep to themselves, put in their time, and go home. School, for them, is a job, not a calling. Others are like "bad-news bumblebees": You can count on them to go from teacher to teacher bemoaning how bad things are and how morale is at an all-time low. Some teachers have goodwill but don't really want to be in the spotlight. They are generally positive, try to stay away from the bad-news bumblebees, put in long hours to get the job done, and don't complain. And in every building, there are teacher leaders. Some lead positively, and some lead negatively. The most successful principals minimize the effect of the negative leaders and harness the energy of the positive leaders to guide the faculty in a productive manner.

Most schools have some type of leadership team or school improvement team. The members are typically department heads or team leaders. The function of the members in most of these groups is to transmit information from the teachers to the administration and from the administration to the teachers. These are typically lifetime appointments; vacancies occur due to retirement or relocation. Slots are filled with those who are willing to do it, not necessarily by those who have the desire to lead or who are the most capable. The discussion topics are usually related to management issues, not to learning and teaching. The minutes of these meetings often describe the same conversations repeated year after year. Instructional changes coming out of these groups are rare, unless the principal reports that the school board office has issued a mandate for all schools to follow.

One of the first things I did after the initial year at my current school was to create the opportunity for a staff council. I say "create the opportunity" because the staff actually created the staff council, not I. If they didn't want it, we wouldn't have one. All I did was ask each department (including custodial and secretarial) in the school to select a representative. Once the council was formed, the only directions I gave the members were to select a leader for the group and to come up with solutions for noninstructional concerns. I did this mainly for two reasons. First, I wanted staff leaders in the building to come up with solutions rather than just report problems to the administration. Second, I wanted the discussions of the department head group to focus on instructional issues, not the day-to-day operation of the school. No administrator would meet with the staff council unless invited to address a certain topic. I have found the procedure of having staff members address schoolwide concerns to be very productive. It's awkward to complain in the faculty lounge about the way things are while sitting next to the people who made the decision. The members of the staff council are definitely in the right seats.

I couldn't say the same about my former instructional leadership team. This team was made up of department heads who represented various subjects. They were all good teachers who worked hard. Their main function as the team was communication. I was the main speaker at every meeting. Conversations were friendly but typically unproductive. Some department heads were there because they were the only people in their departments who were willing to be on the committee. On the other hand, there were strong instructional leaders who were not part of the group. They were respected by their colleagues and were experimenting with novel approaches to learning.

One year, I decided to shake things up. After discussing my concerns with the existing department heads and my administrative team, I announced to the faculty that the department head group was being disbanded. A new School Improvement Team would take its place. I shared the qualities and responsibilities of the group that my previous department heads and my administrative team developed. Anyone could sign up for this new team regardless of what they taught. If two science teachers were selected and no mathematics teachers, that was fine. However, I wanted teachers to apply only if they *wanted* to be on the committee, not if they were the only ones in their departments who were *willing* to be on it. More than half of the teachers expressed a desire to be on the team.

Using the criteria that we selected previously, my two assistant principals and my guidance director worked with me to select the members. We individually rated each candidate and then shared the results with each other. In some cases, we all agreed; in others, we did not. We all had an equal vote in the decision. Our main goal was to find strong instructional leaders who would improve our focus on student learning. The selection was difficult because so many strong teachers applied. Some of the former department heads applied and were selected. Some applied and were not selected. Some did not apply.

The result is that now meetings are discussions in which everyone shares. More conversations are held regarding learning and teaching. Members of the School Improvement Team model instruction for others. They are responsible for new teacher training and professional development. They developed the Educational Operating Plan (see Figures 8.1 and 8.2). They evaluated the staff goals that teachers submitted. The right people are now in the right seats. We can now head the bus in the direction of improved learning.

The Right Procedures

Discipline

Even the procedures used to promote effective discipline are different in schools that are learning communities. Schools in which students are suspended before alternatives are considered do not place a high value on learning. Students who get suspended from school are often doing poorly academically. Suspension causes them to receive zeros, and this gives them less hope of catching up, thus decreasing their desire to be in school. Of course, students who jeopardize the safety of other students and staff need to be removed from the environment. However, those who skip class or are frequently tardy shouldn't be suspended. Students who aren't prepared for class shouldn't be sent to a time-out room. Other than in extreme cases, the first thought should be, "How can we keep him in school?" not "How can we get him out of here?" Often, it merely takes creative thinking on the part of the school staff. We need to increase learning time, not take it away. After-school detention and Saturday school can maintain academic learning time while also acting as a deterrent for inappropriate behavior.

FIGURE 8.1
Tabb Middle School Educational Operating Plan 2004–2005: Student Achievement

Category	Student Achievement
Evidence of Need	• 40% of the students with disabilities passed the SOL English test (21% below AMO). • 35% of the students with disabilities passed the SOL mathematics test (24% below AMO). • 12% of fall semester tests taken were <70, 14% of spring semester tests taken were <70.
Objectives	• To increase the percentage of students with disabilities who pass the Mathematics and Reading/Language Arts SOL tests to at least meet AMO. • To increase academic achievement for all students.
Strategies	• Students who "bring up grades" (BUGS) received recognition along with the students who made all *A*s. • Students who were not successful will be placed in the Red Zone program to receive individual or small-group instruction. • Quarterly/semester and SOL tests will be analyzed for all students to determine areas of weakness. • A peer-tutoring program will be implemented in conjunction with the Red Zone program. • The Earn Your Stripes program will be implemented to reward students involved with the Red Zone program. • All teachers will set academic data-driven goals each semester. • Opportunities for African American students to excel will be analyzed by comparing the percentage of AA students in the school versus the percentage of AA students in advanced programs.
Assessment	BUGS rolls, Red Zone attendance, semester test/quarterly test performance, peer-tutoring contact hours, and the number of "stripes" given to recognize the participation of disabled students in the Red Zone program.
Evidence of Success	By June 2005, students with disabilities will pass the SOL math and English tests at a rate that meets or exceeds AMO. The number of scores below 70 on semester tests will decrease by at least 5%. Average semester test and SOL scores will increase by at least 5%.

Many years ago, being suspended from school meant punishment at home from the parent. Today, suspensions are more like vacations because no adult is home with the student. In addition, because of the inconvenience the parent is alienated from the school rather than being a partner with it. Right or wrong, many parents see the school, rather than their child, as the problem. An effective in-school suspension program or alternative-to-suspension program can increase learning time, take the student out of circulation, and still be undesirable if it's conducted properly. Some say that out-of-school suspension gets the parents involved. However, getting parents involved can be accomplished in other ways. We have found success with what we call the Alternative to Suspension-Isolation (ATS-ISO) program. Students assigned to this program are brought to school by their parents, who also pick them up at the end of the day. The students are required to do schoolwork in carrels, isolated from other students, and they eat lunch in isolation and are escorted to the bathroom as needed. This causes them to be removed from the general student population, but they are doing academic work rather than sleeping or watching television at home. Students suspended from school are often responsible for crimes committed during the

FIGURE 8.2
Tabb Middle School Educational Operating Plan 2004–2005: Instructional Design

Category	Instructional Design
Evidence of Need	Classroom observations revealed that students were watching 37% of the time compared to 35% working and 23% learning.
Objective	To reduce the percentage of students watching and increase the percentage of students in the working and learning categories.
Strategies	**Interactive Notes:** • TMS teachers will be trained in Interactive Note-taking skills and how to teach these skills to students. • TMS teachers will train students in Interactive Note-taking skills. • TMS teachers will report to Dr. Beers on the number of times Interactive Note-taking skills are used each quarter. **Common Planning:** • Common planning will count toward teachers' required duty hours. • TMS master schedule will provide for common planning time each week. • TMS teachers will create and coordinate unit lessons during common planning time. • TMS teachers will create common quarter and semester exams. • TMS core and elective teachers will work with special education teachers to share successful methods of teaching students with special needs.

FIGURE 8.2 *(cont.)*

Tabb Middle School Educational Operating Plan 2004–2005: Instructional Design

Strategies	**Evidence of Learning:** • The principal will provide staff development regarding learner observations and categories of student engagement. • Feedback will be given in all post-observation conferences regarding the percentage of students that fall in each category. • Teachers will be encouraged to develop learner plans that focus on all students mastering the objective. • Teachers will use the learner observation form when doing peer observations. • Strategies for checking for group understanding will be shared with teachers. • White boards and flash cards will be used to increase the use of group checking for understanding. • Teachers will be encouraged to include this school goal as part of their individual goals.
Assessment	• Learner observation summaries compiled for all teachers in Excel. • Faculty meeting agendas.
Evidence of Success	• By June 2005, the percentage of watchers will be less than 35% and the percentage of workers and learners will increase to a combined total of at least 60%. • 100% of TMS teachers will be trained in Interactive Note-taking skills. • 50% of TMS teachers will use Interactive Note-taking structure as a teaching tool an average of five times per quarter. • 75% of units taught will be coordinated within subject/grade levels (common planning).

day. Learning communities find ways to keep students in school when at all possible.

Use of Data

Data-driven decision making is prevalent in learning communities. This means more than just setting a school goal of raising SAT scores. Data can come from surveys completed by students, staff, or parents. The data collected should include grade distributions, attendance summaries, discipline records, and standardized test results. We give common quarter and semester tests to all students in all subjects. In most courses, we can chart our improvement for the past four years. Teachers look at the results at the end of each marking period and compare their students' results to those of past students, as well as to those of students at the same grade level and taking the same class. This analysis occurs for each question on the assessment. All teachers complete a brief form (Figure 8.3) that asks them to list the questions that students missed most often and why they think that happened. Figure 8.4 shows how an entire department can analyze areas of weakness based on the results of common assessments. The assessments are formal, but changing instruction based on the results is an example of assessment *for* learning, not just *of* learning. The goal is not only to collect data but also to improve learning based on the results.

Goal Setting

Each teacher sets at least two data-driven goals each year. One of the goals is per semester and must be academic in nature. The other goal can come from one of the other areas that are included in the goals of the school division. The goal statement should state the evidence of need, the strategies to accomplish the goal, and the evidence of success. At the end of the year, teachers assess their progress in regard to their goals. Some teachers meet their goals; some do not. The important part of the process is the analysis: Teachers who don't meet their goals determine why and develop a plan of action for the next cycle. They get together and establish data-driven goals for their departments. Members of the School Improvement Team get together and establish data-driven school goals in the form of an Educational Operating Plan. There's a clear connection between the goals of the teachers and those of the department, school, and school division.

Observations and evaluations form another means of gathering and using data. The results of all learner observations are tallied in a spreadsheet that is shared by the administrative team. One of the school goals is to reduce the number of students who are wandering and watching, while increasing the number who are working and learning. Some teacher goals are aligned with this goal. During post-observation conferences, administrators inquire about the progress the teacher is making with her goals. An example of a teacher goal is in Figure 8.5.

FIGURE 8.3
Most Frequently Missed Questions: English

Grade: 6	Semester: Fall	Year: 04–05

Subject: Literature

Question Number	Topic	How Will You Address This Next Fall/Spring?
18	Vocabulary	Add more activities in which word meanings are determined from root words, prefixes, and suffixes.
19	Venn diagrams	Have more practice on interpreting information and the placement of information.
26, 46	Similes, metaphors, and "not here" (NH)	Add practice using the response NH.
35–38	Poetic terms: metaphor, repetition, alliteration, and stanza	Have more practice and better examples on test questions.
40, 45	Syllables	Practice counting and identifying lines with a number marker.
41	Central idea	Have more practice with analyzing and interpreting the main idea.
50	Imagery	Have more practice identifying which sense a line of a poem appeals to while incorporating the NH response.

Subject: English

Question Number	Topic	How Will You Address This Next Fall/Spring?
11	Interrogative sentences	• Practice turning questions into statements and identifying the subject. • Have additional practice in the format of the test.
29 31 33	• "Be" verbs used for helping or linking in sentences • Main verbs • Direct objects	• Practice identifying and writing. • Incorporate diagramming to help with identification of types of verbs.
43	Lay/lie	Have additional practice and usage in sentences.
54–56	Connotation	• Emphasize the study of positive and negative connotation. • Incorporate strategies in writing, additional practice, and review.
70	Diagramming	• Have more practice in conjunction with each unit. • Have students constantly review this skill. [Note: Whiteboards are great for this.]

Source: Cindy Evans.

FIGURE 8.4
Analysis of Social Studies Results

Our lowest areas of performance were in the following:
American History to 1877
- Identify a European country's characterization of colonial America (59%).
- Identify the event that allowed the United States to acquire a specific state (60%).

American History 1877 to present
- Identify the results of urbanization (70%).
- Describe the result of specific legislation (71%).

Civics & Economics
- Interpret an economic concept (76%).
- Interpret a political cartoon (67%).

Geography: Identify events of the Civil War (67%).

Our highest areas of performance were in the following:
American History to 1877: Identify a common cause from the specific historical figures involved (96%).

American History 1877 to present: Identify the time of entry of the United States into a specific war (93%).

Civics & Economics
- Analyze a picture illustrating a political system (95%).
- Identify an area from its characteristics (97%).

Geography: Use pictures to describe early American dwellings (94%).

Summary:
As a department, our areas of strength lie in analyzing pictures, the time line of wars, and early American dwellings.

Areas of weakness include analyzing political cartoons and the European perspective of Colonial America, and identifying Civil War events from a geographical map.

As a department, we should continue using graphics and charts on our tests. For improvement, we should have students use maps and geography to predict historical events. We should also spend more time in Civics and Economics on political cartoons. Last, we should try to review Colonial America more in World Studies, if possible.

Source: Michelle Leonard.

FIGURE 8.5
Sample Staff Goals Results Chart

Name:	
Area	**Academic Achievement**
Evidence of Need	13% of my students last year did not pass the first semester test.
Strategies	• Identified areas of difficulty were practiced by students until mastery was achieved. • Group checking for understanding replaced calling on the first hand up. • Students were told what they could expect to learn each day. • Tests were redesigned to incorporate higher levels on Bloom's taxonomy.
Evidence of Success	10% of my students did not pass the semester test.
Comments	• I feel that spending more time with areas of difficulty caused the scores to improve. However, students didn't perform well on the higher-level questions, so this is an area where I need to concentrate in the future. • I feel that the unit tests greatly improved and students learned how to answer critical thinking questions instead of simple multiple-choice questions. • The ability levels of students were not as high this year as in the previous year, in terms of reading. It will be interesting to see several years' worth of data to determine the extent of success.
Area	**Your Choice: Technology**
Evidence of Need	Only 10 parents were e-mailed on a regular basis, and no mass e-mails were sent to the team. (Communication was through handouts sent home.)
Strategies	• Create a database of all students' parents' e-mail addresses. • Send out notices regarding tests, extra credit opportunities, and any other necessary announcements.
Evidence of Success	• A folder was created on my hard drive to accommodate e-mails. More than 200 e-mails from parents were responded to between January 31 and May 15. • Monthly e-mails were sent to parents in regard to projects.
Comments	• In regard to parent communication, having a mass distribution list was helpful in communicating general announcements. I plan to continue this next year.

Reciprocal evaluations are encouraged. Many teachers have their students give them feedback periodically throughout the year. Every two years, I ask the teachers to anonymously evaluate me at the end of the year. The form I use is in Figure 8.6. The leader of the staff council tallies the evaluation and sends the results directly to my supervisor. I use this feedback, along with the other data I gather that address school board goals, to help guide my own goal setting (see Figure 8.7). Once again, the purpose of gathering data is for continuous improvement—for the student, the teacher, the principal, for everyone.

FIGURE 8.6
Sample Principal-Evaluation Form for Teachers

	Excellent	Good	Average	Fair	Poor	N/A
Instructional leadership						
Rapport with students						
Rapport with parents						
Involvement with staff development						
Appropriate setting of priorities						
Professional ethics						
Overall attitude						
Support for teachers						
Listening to others' concerns						
Involving others in decision making						
Promoting positive student discipline						
Conveying high expectations						
Setting an example for others to follow						
Enhancing the community's perception of the school						
Quality of post-observation feedback						
Encouraging continuous school improvement						
Modeling effective teaching techniques						
Encouraging the use of technology						
Visibility						
Using data for decision making						
Providing necessary materials and supplies						
Overall effectiveness as a principal						

Comments: _____

FIGURE 8.7
Barry Beers's Personal-Professional Targets: 2003–2004 Results

PART 1: PERSONAL GROWTH AREAS

Reading: I read *The Differentiated Classroom, Differentiation That Works,* and *Classroom Instruction That Works.* I watched the ASCD video series about differentiation and the one about assessment.

Conferences: I attended the VASCD conference.

Writing: I had an article published in *Principal Leadership* regarding learner observations.

Presentations: I presented at the VASCD and VAESP conferences about learner observations.

PART 2: SUPERINTENDENT'S INITIATIVES

Classroom Observations and Instructional Leadership: To promote effective instruction, I
- Provided inservice training for my faculty on effective instruction and modeled effective instruction techniques during faculty meetings.
- Observed all teachers in the building at least once.
- Provided two formal observations for one-third of the faculty, while my two assistant principals observed the other two-thirds.
- Met with department heads on a regular basis to discuss instructional issues.
- Met with individual departments during the year as needed.

Community Service: I provided community service by adopting a highway and by participating in the American Heart Walk.

Distance Learning: I continued to attempt to find suitable candidates for the Virtual High School and checked on how my students were doing during the year.

PART 3: DATA-DRIVEN PROFESSIONAL GOALS

Six 8th grade students who are either minorities or disabled had a combined total of 22 *F*s and 41 discipline referrals last year. I met with them on a regular basis to assist them in improving their achievement and behavior. The number of discipline referrals dropped from 41 to 17. The number of *F*s dropped from 22 to 7. However, three of the students moved during the 4th quarter, so the results are somewhat skewed. I think my intervention had a direct result on their improved behavior. I do not feel as confident regarding their academic performance.

The Culture

The people and the procedures in schools determine the culture. Striving for continuous improvement doesn't mean changing everything all at once. Senge (1990) describes a condition called *dynamic equilibrium* that involves holding on to or letting go of certain beliefs, assumptions, and certainties. This is the way I think about a learning community. Certain rituals remain that give a school its character and its reputation, way beyond its test scores and the success of its football team. These include the murals on the wall, the teacher who was in the same classroom for 30 years, the way teachers dress, how they treat the students, and what expectations they have for student behavior and academic performance. School leaders should acknowledge and appreciate these characteristics.

At the same time, they should examine what conditions in the school hinder learning. Many reports chronicle the importance of the principal in the success of the school. However, the teachers also have a great impact on the culture of the school. New teachers get their cues from veteran teachers. They see what time the veterans get to school, what they wear, how they react in staff meetings, and how they treat their students. The key to school improvement is to start with a small group of teachers of goodwill. Effective principals involve them with school improvement efforts and listen to their feedback. Whatever works for them can be gradually expanded to the rest of the faculty. If something doesn't catch on for them, it's best discarded or postponed. The key to success is momentum: If a large part of the faculty believes in having learner labs rather than lecture halls, it's easier to sway the reluctant teacher who wants to lecture the students to death. If there are only a handful of believers, however, it's best to retreat and plan another angle of attack.

The principal should be the director of learning. He should model effective instruction and, after providing a safe environment, make student learning his top priority. He should surround himself with competent, hard-working people and then help them do their jobs. If he has to be the boss, something is wrong; a transformational leader is the most powerful because he causes those around him to be more powerful. If he has done a good job, the school should still run smoothly and continue to prosper in his absence.

Celebrate Staff Success

Prior to this point, I have mentioned strategies to help students and staff improve. However, it's vitally important in an organization to stop periodically and celebrate success and show appreciation for the hard work that caused that success. This is an area in which I have improved over the years, but I still have some way to go. My own motivation comes from within, and I am somewhat uncomfortable with public praise. I must keep in mind that everyone wants and needs positive reinforcement. This is true for students and staff.

Teachers need to know when they are doing a good job. This acknowledgment must include more than their getting a pen or coffee cup during Teacher Appreciation Week. The purpose of a walk-through should be twofold. First, as mentioned in Chapter 5, it gives the observer a snapshot of what is occurring in classrooms. Second, and of equal importance, is the opportunity to highlight a positive event caused by the teacher. The follow-up note that I provide after the walk-through is always specific and positive. I resist the temptation to provide a recommendation, which can leave the wrong impression with the teacher. It wouldn't be unlikely for the teacher to focus on what was wrong, in the eyes of the observer, rather than on what was right. I don't want to take that chance. Reflection on the part of the teacher is extremely important, but the observer has to be very careful how she facilitates that process.

Another way to provide positive reinforcement for teachers is to review the results of the previous year with teachers in the first faculty meeting. All too often, principals share what needs to improve without celebrating the success that occurred the year before. I typically use a PowerPoint presentation to show results from the previous three years regarding test scores, discipline summaries, and survey results. I also take this opportunity to show the tally of student behaviors recorded during observations. At the end, I share my vision of the future. The emphasis, however, is clearly on what we accomplished as a faculty.

My experience is that central office staff and principals often focus on teachers who have high failure rates or low test results. But how often do the teachers whose students perform well get recognized? To honor the Teachers of the Year is nice, but this award is rarely based on student performance. During the year, I send personal notes to teachers whose students have shown consistently positive results. I use test scores rather than grades because the awarding of grades is too subjective. When I collect plans throughout the year, I meet with those teachers who are not meeting expectations. However, I also commend those who have exemplary plans.

I have heard teachers "commend" their principal by saying, "He is a good principal; he lets us teach." This situation is common in many schools. If teachers keep their students under control and the parents happy, they don't get too much attention from the administration. This condition drove me out of the classroom. I kept parents happy, and survived year after year with the same activities that kept the students busy and under control, but I wasn't challenged. This is the reason that many teachers either leave the profession or stay in the same rut until they reach retirement. Some teachers have asked me why the expectations that I have are different from those of other principals. They question whether that's fair. My response is that I can't speak for other principals but that my expectations are high because the quality of the faculty and students is so high. I inform my faculty that I wouldn't insult them with low expectations. I firmly believe in the statement that "no one rises to low expectations." The key to success is to provide the support and encouragement to help them meet those expectations.

When my faculty evaluates me (as mentioned earlier in the chapter), two of the first ratings I review are "Conveying high expectations" and "Support for teachers" (see Figure 8.6). The only responses that I find acceptable are that I convey high expectations and have a high level of support for teachers. I have found that one of the most motivating experiences for teachers is to be challenged and to meet that challenge. It's not uncommon for a teacher to hunt me down to share her joy after seeing the results of a semester test. To realize that she met her goal gives her more satisfaction than any trinket I could purchase for her.

I sent the following e-mail to all staff at the end of the first semester in order to commend their success but also to challenge them to improve:

> A few thoughts as the first semester comes to a close. We have all been trained with an emphasis on teaching, not on learning. It's difficult to change our mindset. However, I have seen remarkable progress in the last 3 to 4 years:
>
> - Wandering has almost entirely disappeared.
> - More and more students are working and learning rather than watching the teacher work.
> - Planning, teaching, and assessment are more closely aligned.
> - The textbook has become but one resource, not the curriculum.
> - Objectives now reflect intended student behaviors, not their activities.
> - Students are spending less time copying down information and more time interacting with the information they receive.
>
> My challenge to you for the future is to move up to the next level. Some characteristics of that level include the following:
>
> - "Does anyone know?" is replaced with "How many of you know?"
> - One hand going up to answer a question signals a problem, not a solution.
> - Students are able to tell us what they learned in each class, not just what they did.

Celebrate Student Success

Many schools find ways to celebrate the academic success of top-performing students. Honor rolls can be found posted on walls and Web sites listing students who made all As or all As and Bs. Valedictorians and salutatorians are honored during graduation, along with those in the National Honor Society.

Assistant principal Arty Layne takes the celebration a step further. He initiated a "BUGS" (bringing up grades) program that honors students who show improvement. These students have their names posted next to the honor roll and receive fast-food coupons or free ice cream. Another program that Arty started is "Lunch with the Principal": Students who demonstrate good school citizenship by behaving and doing their best are selected by their teachers to receive a free lunch with the principal in a private setting. Certificates are provided that, we hope, will make it into a scrapbook at home. The students involved in these programs don't typically receive recognition for their accomplishments. They are just good, hard-working kids who might otherwise go unnoticed. If the focus of the school is on learning, then the students who are "getting it" should receive no less attention than those who have demonstrated that they "have it."

Remediation Programs

It's unfortunate that in every school, some students aren't successful. Many schools have extensive remediation programs designed to help students who struggle. To cover this topic in detail would fill another book or two. However, I would like to share a few thoughts in this regard.

Too often, our attempts to help students who fall behind are exactly what we call them: *remediation*. This term typically suggests a process that involves reviewing content that learners didn't master the first time around. My concern is that this is often very time-consuming and doesn't necessarily prepare students for the future. After this treatment, they return to their classes no better equipped for success than before. I prefer the term *acceleration* because it causes us to focus on what those students need in order to catch up. A prime example of remediation is to have slower students continue to work on multiplication and division while their peers tackle real-world applications. In order to accelerate their learning, however, we should provide calculators for the slower students and have them work the same problems. When they get on the job, they will probably be using calculators anyway.

I often find that there is little or no teacher-to-teacher communication from school to school or even between grade levels. Students in the 10th grade have experts in the school who taught them in the 9th grade. However, both sets of teachers rarely share their knowledge. It takes a long time to get to know what works for a student, but that information is lost at the end of the school year and a different teacher starts fresh the following fall. Special education students are an exception to this situation because at least some documentation follows them from year to year, if the teachers choose to look at it. There is some discussion that all students should have a plan that addresses how they learn and that is reviewed and revised each year.

We have found moderate success with a program entitled "Red Zone." Students are in the Red Zone when they aren't succeeding academically. These students are identified during the summer based on their previous performances. At least one day a week is set aside for them to stay after school to receive help from their teachers. The help they receive is a combination of skills needed for the short term and those needed for the long term. In some cases, they may receive help for a test scheduled for the next day. Sometimes, they may receive help with basic skills that they will need for the future. There is much emphasis on application rather than memorization. In some situations, they rotate between teachers from a variety of subject areas to address their specific deficiencies. Their progress is checked frequently during the school year. Students who reach a satisfactory level are placed in the Yellow Zone, where their progress is monitored occasionally and the services are reduced. Other students are added to the Red Zone during the year if their academic performances aren't satisfactory. Administrators and counselors track their attendance in the Red Zone and communicate frequently with their parents.

As mentioned earlier in the chapter, all attention in a learning community should be on the people, procedures, and culture that will improve student achievement and cause continuous improvement for all involved. Chapter 9 discusses recommendations for making this happen and areas needing further research.

What's the Point?

- It's better to spend time getting and keeping the right teachers than to try changing the wrong teachers.
- A principal must be more than the instructional leader. He also must empower those around him to be instructional leaders.
- Like staffs in other organizations, school staffs should frequently use available data to monitor their progress, celebrate success, and set goals to attack areas needing improvement.

9

Making It Happen

Essential Question: What can be learned by studying the process used at one school where an effort has been made to focus on learning?

In this final chapter, I describe the events that have occurred at the school where I currently serve as principal. I do this not because my school is perfect, but because I think it's important to share real-life examples of what *has* happened rather than merely rely on theory that often describes what *should* or *could* be.

The Past

During each of my first 11 years as a principal, I tinkered more and more with the notion of focusing on learner behaviors, not merely on teacher behaviors. I charted student interactions and discussed the results with teachers during post-observation conferences. I encouraged teachers to use group checking for understanding, but I had few techniques to share with them. There were many good teachers at the school who weren't afraid to use nontraditional approaches, but the emphasis for instruction was still on the techniques used by the teacher, not on mastery of the objective by the students.

Moving to my current school gave me the opportunity to up the ante for many reasons. The majority of the students and their parents made education a top priority. The school was known for having good test scores and had few discipline problems compared to neighboring schools. This allowed me to focus on the big picture rather than putting out the fires that consume the days of many principals. In addition, the majority of the staff was strong and dedicated to providing an optimal learning environment for the students. By all accounts, this was a good school.

My first few years at the school were devoted to renovating the building and to adding 15 new classrooms, a second gymnasium, and a new media center. The entire project was completed while students were in the building. I wouldn't recommend that procedure to anyone. I took this time to observe the current conditions because to introduce anything new during that chaos would be suicidal. It was evident that some of the wrong people were on the bus. In addition, some of the right people had not been challenged to meet high expectations.

Overall, the instructional program was traditional in nature. A few teachers had no plans that I could detect. Many teachers planned for activities that they listed in small squares in the traditional green plan book. A few had detailed plans in word processing documents contained in binders. Most teachers existed in isolation, except for the team meetings, when they discussed the students they taught in common. The interdisciplinary movement had come and gone, so most teachers taught the chapters in their textbooks with little knowledge of what others were doing. For the most part, the invisible walls of subject and grade partitioned teachers in the building. There was little use of data for decision making. The only statistic that was mentioned in previous schoolwide planning was in regard to the number of failures and discipline problems. Classroom observations focused entirely on teacher behaviors.

I decided to gradually attack both ends of the performance continuum at the same time. I knew I had to get some people either off the bus or to the point at which their performances were acceptable. At the same time, I needed to empower those who were willing and able to be taken to a higher level as teachers and leaders. It took me five years to get the first job accomplished. I can now say that every one of the teachers in my school is at least good. The second task was easier but still challenging. Prior to my arrival, "favorite" teachers were asked to share their expertise at faculty meetings and professional development sessions. This divided the faculty to a certain extent. During the early stages, I was careful to work with teachers without putting them in the spotlight. As I conversed with teachers, I shared examples of successful practices that I had seen in classrooms, without identifying the source. Each year, discussions regarding learning and teaching grew in frequency and depth.

My goal was to sell, not tell. I introduced new ideas a few at a time rather than all at once. Each year, I built upon previous content as I introduced new information. The reaction of the teachers guided my emphasis. My goal was to plant seeds and to support any growth that resulted. When I had achieved "critical mass"—that is, acceptance by a large portion of the faculty—I talked about certain practices as though they were part of our culture. For instance, having an activity that grabs the students as they walk in the door caught on quickly. Some teachers called it a "do now" or "bell ringer" or "sponge" activity. The name doesn't matter. It soon became a standard operating procedure, not an innovation. The students are now trained so that they expect it from class to class, year to year.

Having teachers develop acceptable daily objectives (as described in Chapter 2) has been harder to institutionalize. It wasn't until the fourth year that almost all teachers accepted the idea. Even then, putting it into daily practice was difficult to achieve. It made more sense to teachers of mathematics than it did to teachers of electives. Getting teachers to use group checking for understanding is another idea that we were slow to institutionalize. And calling on the first hand up was a hard habit to break.

Below are some of the teacher comments I have heard throughout the years, followed by my reactions:

- **If I keep checking to see who is learning, I won't have time
  to cover the curriculum.** To a noneducator, this might seem
  somewhat absurd—almost like a carpenter saying, "If I keep
  checking to see if the boards are straight, I will never get
  the house built." Even so, this opinion is one of the greatest
  impediments to teaching for learning. Many teachers still feel
  pressured to teach "it" whether the students learn "it" or not.
- **I will know if they learned it on Friday when I give the test.**
  This comment supports the "teach, test, hope for the best"
  philosophy. It illustrates the difference between assessment
  of learning and assessment *for* learning. "Hoping" for positive
  results is not enough. If we don't check along the way, we
  won't make necessary changes to instruction. By Friday, it's
  too late to go back.
- **Some of my objectives take students more than one day to
  master.** Does this mean that they don't have to learn anything the first day? I would agree that goals take longer to
  master and the big questions take longer to answer, but objectives should be accomplished daily. Breaking them down into
  smaller parts makes it easier for students to keep up.
- **So you are saying my students didn't learn anything during
  the lesson?** This comment comes when teachers don't see
  "learner" checked on the observation chart. This is usually
  because the objective is poorly worded or the teacher didn't
  use any form of group checking for understanding. In most
  cases, my response is that the students may have learned
  something, but it wasn't evident that they had. I feel learning
  should be evident, not merely assumed. I define learning as
  the accomplishment of the objective. The teacher who calls
  on the first hand up often assumes the other students have it.
  This practice often results in misleading information.

- **Band and chorus aren't taught the same as math. We have no need for daily objectives. We are creative, spontaneous.** Most teachers feel that their subjects are unique. Teaching practices are often different from class to class, but learning is not. Band teachers could learn a few things from mathematics teachers; mathematics teachers could learn a few things from band teachers. All of the comments made throughout this book about learning apply to all subjects because they apply to all students. Art students are better able to successfully complete projects when they know what they should know and be able to do at the end of each class period. Assigning them a project to be done by the end of the week, without daily checkpoints, will cause many of them to be confused, disorganized, and lacking confidence. A lack of effort often results.

- **In the learning category, I only got 15 percent. Does this mean that 85 percent of the students didn't learn anything?** It was not until I met with teachers in small groups that I discovered this disconnect between what I was saying and what the teachers were hearing. A 15 in the learning category means that 15 percent of the time, students demonstrated mastery of the objective. This is a very acceptable total; you would not expect a much higher number because most of the time, students should be "working" on the way to "learning."

- **What will I do at the beginning of class if I find some of them already know "it"?** At least the teacher is checking. That puts her at the head of the class. This teacher is ready for a discussion of differentiated instruction—not because it's a hot topic, but because she realizes that her students are different. The key is not to wait until the beginning of class to ask the question. Differentiated planning takes time, which most teachers don't have. However, teachers who plan together can share the load. One teacher might plan for the majority of the class, while another two plan for those who get it and those who don't. In any case, differentiated planning doesn't have to occur all at once. Adding 10 or 15 differentiated plans a year is better than having none at all.

- **You say the students are working. I say they are learning.** There are no absolute answers, so we can agree to disagree. This comment will lead to a discussion of the objective and how assessment was performed. Was the stated objective really what the teacher wanted the students to *learn* that day? Quite often, it wasn't. Did the assessment for learning really identify those who demonstrated mastery of the objective? Quite often, it didn't. One teacher, Ronnie Paetz, concluded that whether it was called working or learning didn't matter as much as the conversation we were having. Bingo!

- **I was afraid too many students were "watching" while you were observing my class.** I was pleased that this teacher was thinking about learning after being at the school for only a few months. I am convinced that teachers who think about learning on a regular basis will get better results.

- **You have scarred me for life. Now, whenever I am teaching, I think about whether the students are learning or not.** Fantastic!

The Present

Recent results of observations by administrators identified a decrease in the percentage of wanderers and watchers and an increase in the percentage of workers and learners at my school. Most of these observations were announced. I'm not so naive to assume that teaching for learning, as I have described it, is institutionalized. However, we're moving in that direction.

The assistant principals and I recently used a rubric to check all plan books. We found that approximately 10 percent were unsatisfactory, 80 percent were satisfactory, and 10 percent were exemplary. Most of the unsatisfactory plan books had daily plans but no dates listed. The exemplary plan books had assessments for learning and differentiated instruction listed daily with excellent objectives. Planning for learning has continued to improve each year.

As I look into classrooms (all have interior windows), I'm able to see more students actively engaged. I see more evidence of students using INBs and less copying of notes from the board or overhead. I see much use of whiteboards and increased use of flash cards (though these have been slow to catch on). Fewer students are gazing at the teacher for long periods of time. It's also encouraging to see so many new teachers concentrating on teaching and assessing for learning. Since they all plan with veteran teachers, this causes me to believe that new and veteran teachers are eliminating some traditional practices in favor of teaching for learning.

The small group of teachers I started with has grown in number to the point that meeting higher expectations is the norm, not the exception. In fact, teachers get angry if another teacher doesn't meet the standards that have become part of the culture of the school. Even though the expectations are high, all indicators suggest that teacher morale is also high. A recent anonymous survey conducted by the York Education Association revealed that our school was rated highest in teachers being "professionally treated" and the total "morale index" compared to other secondary schools. I was also pleased to see that we were rated extremely high in "quality of feedback given." This leads me to believe that teachers are buying into the need to have students learn and to have observers look for evidence of learning.

I have hesitated to mention our progress with standardized achievement, because I have read and heard too many educators explain the success of certain programs or techniques based on gains that include small samples or short periods of time. The relationships between various programs and results that are claimed to be causal might in fact be merely correlational. For those of you who need validation through standardized test scores, I can assure you that our results are very high compared to those of other schools and, more important, that we have increased our scores every year.

The Future

Even though we are headed in the right direction, we still have much room for improvement. I continue to see some teachers call on the first hand up and then move on. I would like to see more evidence of students helping students. It doesn't take much time or effort to tell the students to talk to their neighbors and then report what those neighbors think. Some teachers fear a loss of control or don't see this as a productive use of time. We still have activities that creep into our objectives every now and then. I inform teachers that reading a short story is not an objective unless you are going to teach the students to read. Likewise, "understand" and "appreciate" are good verbs for goals but are too broad for daily objectives.

Another area in which we need to improve is assessment. I often find that we're guilty of a condition found in many schools whereby we set lofty goals but assess only at the lower levels of knowledge and comprehension. An example is when the plan calls for students to evaluate or apply, but the majority of the test asks the students to recall the who, what, where, and when. It's unfortunate that tests are often designed for ease of grading rather than assessment of specific objectives.

The day of review prior to the test can also be improved. Games such as bingo and those modeled after the show "Jeopardy!" involve students in a fun review of previously supplied information. The problem is that this information typically is at a low level of comprehension. In addition, easy and difficult questions both get the same amount of attention, rather than students spending more time on the areas of difficulty.

My experience at my own school leads me to make the following recommendations for others.

For teachers interested in teaching for learning:

- Ask yourself some key questions to determine how you can improve.

- Do you have a solid foundation regarding current research about learning?
- Do you think students are more like empty vessels to be filled or seeds to be cultivated?
- What guides your true curriculum? Is it the text, your county or state curriculum, or something else?
- Do you assess learning before, during, and after instruction? If so, how?
- Do you plan, teach, and assess for various differences among students, or do you use "one size fits all"?

- Do a little at a time. Find time to put together a few good plans and then add as you go. Revise a few tests, and make them match the intended outcomes. You can change the others later.
- Remove yourself from isolation. Don't wait for someone else to take the lead. Invite a teacher to your classroom, and she might do the same for you. Talk about the instruction and the learning that was evident. Plan with other teachers as much as possible. Three heads are better than one!

For principals:

- If you're new to a building, go slowly. Ask the faculty and staff to share their perceptions of both the strengths and the areas needing improvement long before you make any decisions in the absence of this information. Too many principals march into the first faculty meeting armed with how they do it without seeking first to find out how the people in the building have done it. This is similar to the teachers checking for prior knowledge before teaching a lesson. The staff needs to know right away that its opinions are valued.
- Let the data guide your decision making. What do the surveys tell you? What data are available regarding student performance? Teacher performance? Post your yearly results in a

prominent place in your office and throughout the school. Let visitors to your office know that continuous improvement is a high priority for you and your school. Some offices I visit are filled with pictures of sports teams and athletic trophies; others are filled with charts, books, and periodicals providing information about academic achievement.

- Don't let putting out fires consume your time so that you can't take care of the bigger issues. You have to take time to get the wrong people off the bus. It takes a great deal of time at first, but doing so saves you time in the long run. You have to get into classrooms. Set a schedule for classroom observations, and stick to it. If you don't, there will always be something that comes up to distract you. I have found that by sticking to my observation schedule, the other tasks somehow get taken care of. Sometimes, this means others need to assume more responsibility while you are in a classroom or conferencing with a teacher. This is not a bad thing.

- Model the instructional procedures that you expect from your teachers. If you don't want them to stand and deliver, don't subject them to that at faculty meetings.

- Observe for learning. The method you choose isn't as important as the focus. Don't give in regarding the use of daily objectives.

- Check what you expect. Share your expectations for planning, and collect plans from all teachers periodically.

- Reinforce the positives, and remove the negatives. This is in regard to people and procedures.

- Achieve critical mass. Increase the percentage of staff moving in the right direction.

For supervisors of principals:

- Ask principals how many of their teachers shouldn't be on the bus. Provide support and encouragement for them until all people on the bus are good or better.

- Model the instructional procedures that you expect your principals to model for their teachers. Don't hold a three-hour meeting in which you lecture about effective instructional strategies.
- Help principals be instructional leaders through professional development and through observation followed by specific feedback. Observe how they perform classroom observations and teacher conversations. Observe faculty meetings.
- Facilitate the collection of data, and help principals to understand the data and see how the data collected at their schools address the goals of the school division. Encourage principals to gather data from each teacher and each classroom to determine how those data address school goals.
- Share an expectation for learning to be evident in every classroom, in every school, on a daily basis.
- Bring in someone from the outside who can perform a learning audit for a school or school division. This is done for finance, curriculum, and management. Is learning not as important?

Throughout this book, I have illustrated the fact that, although much new information is available regarding how people learn, traditional teaching methods still dominate classroom practice. In order for this to change, teachers, teacher trainers, and teacher supervisors need to accept the belief that students should demonstrate learning each day, in every class. I firmly believe that, in the vast majority of schools, the right people are on the bus. We just need to drive the bus toward learning.

What's the Point?

- Progress might be very slow, but continuous improvement is the key to success. Getting started is the first step.
- The goal should be to get a critical mass of teachers to focus on learning so that those who don't will feel peer pressure to get on board.

- Evidence of learning should be the focus for all teachers, all principals, and all supervisors of principals in order for students to be prepared for the world ahead of them.

Appendix A ~ Sample Learner Plan for Mathematics

Title: Line Plots, Frequency Tables, and Histograms		Content Area: Mathematics 7
Grade Level: 7	Date: March 3, 2005	SOL: 7.17, 7.18
Assignments: pp. 6–7 (1–7, 9–21)	SOL Review/Warm-up Problems: Determine the mean, median, mode, and range of the following data: 1, 4, 7, 9, 5, 4, 8 *(mean: 5.4; mode: 4; median: 5; range: 8)*.	

Lesson Objective: TSWBAT collect, organize, display, and interpret data using line plots, frequency tables, and histograms.

Check for Prior Knowledge: Students will create a line plot, frequency table, and histogram to display the following data: *Number of pets per household:* 0, 0, 2, 1, 3, 2, 0, 3, 2.

Student Engagement:
- SOL review and check.
- Check homework: pp. 19–20 (1–7, 10–11).
- Students will self-assess their current knowledge regarding line plots, frequency tables, and histograms by showing one to five fingers (1 = no knowledge; 5 = completely understand).

Initial Activity:
- Students will explain what it means to tally information. Review the five tally marks with them. Students will describe situations in which they have used the process of tallying. Students will get with a partner and solve the coded message QCF FJDXF CJR XJWZFZ using the clues shown on the overhead. Students who solve the code will explain how they got the answer *(The Eagle has landed)*. Explain that when they figured out how many times a letter occurred, they used the concept of frequency.
- Hand out Displaying Frequency Notes. Explain the uses of and how to create a line plot, frequency table, and histogram. Students will highlight the key elements of each in their notes. Go through the examples in the notes, talking about the similarities and differences of each type of graph. Students will assist me in creating each type of graph using the letters per word in *The Eagle has landed.*
- After each guided practice, students will fill out the Try It Out section of their notes using the phrase "Today is the day yesterday would have been if tomorrow would have been today." Walk around and assist students. When the students are finished, go over the answers with the class.

Closure:
- Each student will say his or her birthday month while I tally it on the overhead. Students will work with a partner to create a line plot, frequency table, and histogram of the data. Volunteers will share with the class. Compare and contrast each:
  - *Compare:* all have titles, data represented, display information
  - *Contrast:* each looks different (line plot: visual display of X; frequency table: shows numbers; histogram: shows intervals)
- Students will do another self-assessment of their knowledge.

(continued on the next page)

Appendix A ~ Sample Learner Plan for Mathematics (*cont.*)

Assessment of Learning (Formal)	Assessment for Learning (Informal)	Resources (Text/Technology)	Differentiation
X Check and correct homework X Student drill __ Quiz __ Test __ Presentation __ Project __ Written report __ Other:	X Observation X Walk around X Signaling X Choral response X Class work X Oral questioning X Discussion X Other (interactive notes):	X P.H. Course 2 Text, pp. 4–7 __ VA SOL, Math 8, Lapinski __ Buckle Down on VA Math __ Calculators X Overhead X Manipulative: X TV/VCR X PowerPoint X Internet X Instructional software __ Other:	X Cooperative learning X Paired activity __ Reduced # questions X Other (interactive notes) X Varied grouping X Choice __ Movement X Manipulatives X Contract X Think/pair/share __ Other:

Power Strategies/Activities	Observations/Recommendations for Future Use
X Setting objectives and providing feedback X Questions, cues, and advance organizers X Identifying similarities and differences X Cooperative learning X Nonlinguistic representations X Note taking and summarizing X Reinforcing effort and providing recognition X Homework and practice X Generating and testing hypotheses	

Source: Ginny Tonneson.

Appendix B ~ Sample Learner Plan for Physical Education

Title: Stickwork/Dribbling		**Content Area:** Field Hockey #1
Grade Level: 8	**Date:** April 26, 2005	**SOL:** 8.2a

Lesson Objectives: TSWBAT	**Resources/Equipment:**
• Grip and manipulate the stick using the correct hand position. • Perform stickwork drills to improve eye-hand coordination. • Differentiate between a controlled dribble and a loose dribble; explain when to use each. • Perform the reverse stick to keep the ball on the right side of the body.	• 40 sticks • 20 balls • Marked field

Student Engagement: Students will

- Perform warm-up exercises, and answer the following: How many of you have played some form of hockey? Are on the school team? What are some of the differences between the different types of hockey?
- Listen to an explanation of safety rules: 2 hands and 2 players; high stick above the waist. Using the correct grip will help ensure safety.
- Jog the football field, partner and label as #1 or #2. After jog, get stick and ball.
- Perform stickwork drills: toe to toe, quick taps, and under the stick. 20 sec. each, students count their own results. Drills are done daily to allow students to improve.
- Shuttle dribble with partner using a controlled dribble. Shuttle dribble with partner using the loose dribble. Students assess which one is more difficult for them.
- Perform the figure 8 dribble with spots.
- Turn in equipment, and answer the following questions with their partners: Which hand goes on top? What is a reverse dribble? What is the difference between a controlled dribble and a loose dribble? When should you use each?

Assessment of Learning	**Assessment for Learning**	**Differentiation**
___ Quizzes ___ Skills tests ___ Written test ___ Homework ___ Project	___ Observation _X_ Choral response ___ Signaling ___ Oral questions ___ Discussion _X_ Whiteboards	_X_ Modified activity _X_ Paired activities ___ Peer teaching _X_ Think/pair/share ___ Lead-up activities ___ Flexible grouping by readiness ___ Modified rules by readiness _X_ Modified equipment by readiness _X_ Demonstration stations ___ Other:

Observations/Recommendations for Future Use
Identify school team's field hockey players to help with demonstrating skills. SWD use a bigger, lighter ball.

Source: Kay Aultman.

Appendix C ~ Sample Unit Plan for Social Studies

1/30/04 Describe the basic structure of the national legislative branch (NLB) and define relevant terms. (Test items #18, 19, 27)

2/02/04 Explain the function of the NLB, define relevant terms, and review the basic structure of the NLB. (Test items #1 and 2)

2/03/04 List the powers of Congress and define relevant terms. (Test items #7–11)

2/04/04 Explain the role of committees in Congress and define relevant terms. (Test items #5, 12, 13)

2/05/04 Describe the leadership in Congress, define relevant terms, and review the basic structure and function of the NLB for a quiz. (Test item #28)

2/06/04 Compare and contrast the two houses of Congress. (Test items #33, 34, 36)

2/09/04 Demonstrate mastery over the basic structure and function of the NLB and relevant terms via a quiz. (Test items #1, 2, 18, 19, 27)

2/10/04 Explain and analyze the lawmaking process at the national level of government by learning the steps of a bill through the House of Representatives and review for quiz on powers of Congress, role of committees in Congress, leadership in Congress, and comparison and contrast between the two houses of Congress. (Test items #5, 7–13, 28, 33, 34, 36, 44–55)

2/11/04 Explain and analyze the lawmaking process at the national level of government by learning the steps of a bill through the Senate. (Test items #48–51)

2/12/04 Explain and analyze the lawmaking process at the national level of government by learning the purpose of a conference committee and the final approval in the lawmaking process. (Test items #52–54)

2/13/04 Explain what happens to a bill once it is forwarded to the U.S. president and Congress's response. (Test item #55)

2/16/04 Demonstrate mastery of the powers of Congress, role of committees in Congress, leadership in Congress, and comparison and contrast of two houses of Congress. (Test items #5, 7–13, 28, 33, 34, 36)

2/17/04 Describe the basic structure of the state legislative branch (SLB). (Test items #16, 21, 31)

2/18/04 Explain the function of the SLB. (Test items #24–26, 30, 35, 37–39)

2/19/04 Compare and contrast the state and national legislative branches, and review for a quiz on the lawmaking process at the national level of government. (Test items #3, 23, 32, 42, 43, 56–66)

Appendix C ~ Sample Unit Plan for Social Studies (*cont.*)

2/20/04	Demonstrate mastery of the lawmaking process in Congress. (Test items #44–55)
2/23/04	Explain and analyze the lawmaking process in the Virginia General Assembly by learning the steps of a bill through the House of Delegates. (Test items #44–47)
2/24/04	Explain and analyze the lawmaking process in the Virginia General Assembly by learning the steps of a bill through the state Senate. (Test items #48–54)
2/25/04	Explain and analyze the lawmaking process in the Virginia General Assembly by learning the purpose of a conference committee and final approval. (Test items #52–54, 55)
2/26/04	Explain what happens to a bill once it is forwarded to the governor and the General Assembly's response. (Test item #55)
2/27/04	Review for a quiz over the basic structure and function of the SLB, and compare and contrast the state and national legislative branches. (Test items #16, 21, 24–26, 29–31, 35, 37–39, and 3, 23, 32, 42, 43, 56–66)

Source: Mary Norris.

Appendix D ~ Sample Percents Unit Plan for Mathematics

SOL	Test Question Number	Date	Objective: The Student Will Be Able to (TSWBAT) . . .
8.1	1–3	3/2	• Convert a percent to a fraction. • Convert a percent to a decimal. • Match percents to equivalent fractions and decimals.
8.1	4–6	3/3	• Convert fractions to percents. • Convert decimals to percents.
8.17	7–12	3/4	• Solve problems by using proportions. • Solve problems that require the use of a formula. • Substitute values for variables in a formula.
8.17	7–12	3/5	• Write and solve percent equations. • Use equations to solve percent problems.

8.17
8.1
	7–12	3/8	Review for quiz:
			  • Use proportions to find part of a whole.
			  • Use proportions to find whole amount.
			  • Use proportions to write and solve percent.
			  • Complete chart of equivalent decimal, percent, and
			    fractions.

8.17
8.1
		3/9	Quiz: Demonstrate mastery of
			  • Setting up equation and solving for missing part using
			    proportions.
			  • Completing chart of missing fractions, decimals, or
			    percents.

8.17	7–12	3/10	Solve word problems by using proportions.
8.17	13	3/11	• Solve practical problems by using computational procedures. • Calculate the percent of change.

		3/12	Quiz: Demonstrate mastery of
			  • Solving word problems using proportions.
			  • Calculating percent of change.

8.17	14	3/15	Solve problems involving discount.
8.3	15	3/16	Solve problems involving discount and tipping.
8.17	16	3/17	Calculate simple interest.

Appendix D ~ Sample Percents Unit Plan for Mathematics (*cont.*)

8.17 8.3 8.1		3/18	Short quiz: Demonstrate knowledge of • Calculating discount, tip, and simple interest. Review for test: • Changing decimals and fractions to percents. • Changing percents to decimals and fractions. • Using proportions to find part, whole, or percent. • Calculating percent of change. • Calculating discount, tip, and simple interest.
8.17 8.3 8.1		3/19	Test: • Changing decimals and fractions to percents. • Changing percents to decimals and fractions. • Using proportions to find part, whole, or percent. • Calculating percent of change. • Calculating discount, tip, and simple interest.

Source: Heather Vaden.

Appendix E ~ Sample Fractions Unit Plan for Mathematics

SOL	Test Question Number	Date	Objective: The Student Will Be Able to (TSWBAT) . . .
6.3a 6.3a	6–10	10/16	• List the multiples of a number. • Find the least common multiple (LCM) between two numbers. • Find common denominators between two fractions.
6.3b	9–10	10/17	• List the factors of a number. • Find common denominators between three or more fractions.
7.1b 7.1f	5	10/20	• Compare fractions that have common denominators. • Order fractions that have common denominators.
7.1b 7.1b 7.1f	1–4 6–8 9–10	10/21	• Find equivalent fractions. • Compare fractions that do not have common denominators. • Order fractions that do not have common denominators.

7.1b
7.1b, f
		10/22	Review for quiz:
			  • Find equivalent fractions.
			  • Compare and order fractions.

		10/23	Quiz: Demonstrate mastery of finding equivalent fractions and comparing and ordering fractions.
6.3c, d		10/24	Identify prime numbers and composite numbers.
6.3	11–13	10/27	Find the prime factorization of a number.
6.3b	11–13	10/28	Find the greatest common factor (GCF) using prime factorization.

		10/29	Quiz: Demonstrate mastery of
			  • Comparing and ordering fractions.
			  • Finding the prime factorization of a number.
			  • Using the prime factorization of a number to find the GCF.

6.6b	14–18	10/30	Simplify fractions.
6.6a	21–22 19–20	10/31	• Convert a mixed number into an improper fraction. • Convert an improper fraction into a mixed number.
7.1a	23–32	11/3	Convert decimals to fractions and fractions to decimals.

		11/4	Review for test:
			  • Compare and order fractions.
			  • Use the prime factorization of a number to find the GCF.
			  • Reduce a fraction to simplest form.
			  • Convert decimals to fractions and fractions to decimals.

Appendix E ~ Sample Fractions Unit Plan for Mathematics (*cont.*)

		11/5	Test: Demonstrate mastery of • Comparing and ordering fractions. • Using the prime factorization of a number to find the GCF. • Reducing a fraction to simplest form. • Converting decimals to fractions and fractions to decimals.

Source: Melissa Moore.

References

Acheson, K., & Gall, M. (1980). *Techniques in the clinical supervision of teachers*. New York: Longman.

Adams, R. S., & Biddle, B. J. (1970). *Realities of teaching: Exploration with videotape*. New York: Holt, Rinehart, and Winston.

Bandura, A. (1977). *Social learning theory*. New York: General Learning Press.

Black, P., & William, D. (1998, October). Inside the black box: Raising standards through classroom assessment. *Phi Delta Kappan, 80*(2), 139–149.

Bransford, J., Brown, A., & Cocking, R. (Eds.). (2000). *How people learn: Brain, mind, experience, and school*. Washington, DC: National Research Council.

Brooks, J., & Brooks, M. (1993). *The case for constructivist classrooms*. Alexandria, VA: Association for Supervision and Curriculum Development.

Brophy, J., & Good, T. (1970). Brophy-Good system (teacher-child dyadic interaction). In *Mirrors for behavior: An anthology of observation instruments continued* (Vol. A, 1970 supplement). Philadelphia: Research for Better Schools.

Caine, G., & Caine, R. (1994). *Making connections: Teaching and the human brain*. New York: Addison-Wesley.

Chappuis, S., & Stiggins, R. J. (2002). Classroom assessment for learning. *Educational Leadership, 60*(1), 40–44.

Cohen, E. G. (1972). Sociology and the classroom: Setting the conditions for teacher-student interaction. *Review of Educational Research, 42*(4), 441.

Collins, J. (2001). *Good to great*. New York: Harper Business.

Commonwealth of Virginia Board of Education. (2001). *Curriculum framework: Civics and economics* (p. 2). Richmond, VA: Author.

Danielson, C. (1996). *Enhancing professional practice*. Alexandria, VA: Association for Supervision and Curriculum Development.

Edmonds, R. R. (1982, December). On school improvement. *Educational Leadership, 40*(3), 13–15.

Flanders, N. (1970). *Analyzing teaching behavior.* Reading, MA: Addison-Wesley.

Gardner, H. (1983). *Frames of mind.* New York: Basic Books.

Good, T. (1981). Teacher expectations and student perceptions: A decade of research. *Educational Leadership, 38*(5), 415–421.

Halford, J. M. (1998). Easing the way for new teachers. *Educational Leadership, 55*(5), 33–36.

Heller, D. (2004). *Teachers wanted.* Alexandria, VA: Association for Supervision and Curriculum Development.

Hunter, M. (1982). *Mastery teaching: Increasing instructional effectiveness in secondary schools, colleges, and universities.* El Segundo, CA: TIP Publications.

Hurley, V., Greenblatt, R. B., & Cooper, B. S. (2003, May). Transforming conversations: Transforming supervision. *Educational Leadership, 3*(9), 31–36.

Jensen, E. (1998). *Teaching with the brain in mind.* Alexandria, VA: Association for Supervision and Curriculum Development.

Johnson, D., & Johnson, R. (1984). *Circles of learning.* Alexandria, VA: Association for Supervision and Curriculum Development.

Johnson, S., & Kardos, S. (2002). Keeping new teachers in mind. *Educational Leadership, 59*(6), 12–16.

Kagan, S. (1994). *Cooperative learning.* San Clemente, CA: Resources for Teachers, Inc.

Kerman, S. (1979). Teacher expectations and student achievement. *Phi Delta Kappan, 60*(1), 716–718.

Marzano, R., Pickering, D., & Pollock, J. (2001). *Classroom instruction that works.* Alexandria, VA: Association for Supervision and Curriculum Development.

Piaget, J. (1970). *Science of education and the psychology of the child* (D. Coltman, Trans.). New York: Orion Press.

Resnick, L. (1987). *Education and learning to think.* Washington, DC: National Academy Press.

Rowe, M. B. (1972). *Wait-time and rewards as instructional variables: Their influence in language, logic, and fate control.* Paper presented at the National Association for Research in Science Teaching, Chicago. (ERIC Document Reproduction Service No. ED 061 103)

Sadker, D., & Sadker, M. (1986, March). Sexism in the classroom: From grade school to graduate school. *Phi Delta Kappan, 67*(7), 512–515.

Searfoss, L., & Enz, B. (1996). Can teacher evaluation reflect holistic instruction? *Educational Leadership, 53*(6), 38–41.

Senge, P. M. (1990). *The fifth discipline: The art and practice of the learning organization* (p. 371). New York: Currency Doubleday.

Skinner, B. F. (1953). *Science and human behavior.* New York: Macmillan.

Stanford, G., & Roark, A. E. (1974). *Human interaction in education.* Boston: Allyn and Bacon.

Stiggins, J. (2002, June). Assessment crisis: The absence of assessment for learning. *Phi Delta Kappan, 83*(10), 758–765.

Stronge, J. (2002). *Qualities of effective teachers.* Alexandria, VA: Association for Supervision and Curriculum Development.

Thorndike, R. L., & Stein, S. (1937). An evaluation of the attempts to measure social intelligence. *Psychological Bulletin, 34,* 275–285.

Tomlinson, C. A. (1999). *The differentiated classroom: Responding to the needs of all learners.* Alexandria, VA: Association for Supervision and Curriculum Development.

Vygotsky, L. S. (1978). *Mind in society.* Cambridge, MA: Harvard University Press.

Walen, E., & DeRose, M. (1993). The power of peer appraisals. *Educational Leadership, 51*(2), 45–48.

Wiggins, G., & McTighe, J. (1998). *Understanding by design.* Alexandria, VA: Association for Supervision and Curriculum Development.

Wiggins, G., & McTighe, J. (2004). *Understanding by design* (2nd ed.). Alexandria, VA: Association for Supervision and Curriculum Development.

Wong, H., & Wong, R. (1998). *The first days of school: How to be an effective teacher.* Mountain View, CA: Harry K. Wong Publications.

Index

About the Author

 Barry Beers has been a middle and high school administrator for 21 years. In 1988, he received a Doctorate in Educational Administration from the College of William and Mary. His dissertation was titled A *Study of the Relationship Between Student Achievement and Teacher-Student Interaction in Secondary Classrooms*. He also was an adjunct professor at the College of William and Mary and an educational consultant. He was named the Outstanding Principal in Virginia for 1992 to 1994.

Barry has presented at numerous local, state, and national conferences, and in May 2004, he published an article in *Principal Leadership* entitled "Who's Learning" that gathered considerable interest from principals across the country. He has been married to a 1st grade teacher for 32 years and has two daughters, one each teaching 3rd grade and kindergarten, and a son attending college. Barry can be reached by e-mail at bbeers@ycsd.york.va.us.

Related ASCD Resources: Learning-Driven Schools

At the time of publication, the following ASCD resources were available (ASCD stock numbers appear in parentheses). For up-to-date information about ASCD resources, go to www.ascd.org.

Audiotapes

The Adolescent Brain: A Work in Progress (#203164S25), by Patricia Wolfe

Online Courses

Bridging Learning Theory in the Classroom, by Diane L. Jackson

Print Products

Inspiring Active Learning: A Handbook for Teachers, by Merrill Harmin (#194027S25)

The Learning Leader: How to Focus School Improvement for Better Results, by Douglas B. Reeves (#105151S25)

Powerful Learning, by Ron Brandt (#198179S25)

Videotapes

The Brain and Learning Series (four videos, #498062S25)

How to Create an Effective Learning Environment (#498040S25)

For more information: send e-mail to member@ascd.org; call 1-800-933-2723 or 703-578-9600, press 2; send a fax to 703-575-5400; or write to Information Services, ASCD, 1703 N. Beauregard St., Alexandria, VA 22311-1714 USA.